Stanford University

THE CAMPUS GUIDE

Stanford University

second edition

Richard Joncas, David J. Neuman,

and Paul V. Turner

Princeton Architectural Press

NEW YORK | *2006*

Princeton Architectural Press
37 East 7th Street
New York, NY 10003
212.995.9620

For a free catalog of books published by Princeton Architectural Press,
call 1.800.722.6657 or visit www.papress.com

Editor, first edition: Jan Cigliano
Editor, second edition: Nicola Bednarek
Design: Sara E. Stemen
Maps: Jane Sheinman
Special thanks to Nettie Aljian, Dorothy Ball, Janet Behning, Megan Carey, Penny (Yuen Pik) Chu,
Russell Fernandez, Jan Haux, Clare Jacobson, John King, Mark Lamster, Nancy Eklund Later, Linda
Lee, Katharine Myers, Lauren Nelson, Molly Rouzie, Scott Tennent, Jennifer Thompson, Joseph
Weston, and Deb Wood of Princeton Architectural Press —Kevin C. Lippert, publisher

Photo credits:
The publisher thanks photographer Harvey Helfand of Berkeley, California, for his
generosity and talented assistance.
pages ii, 19 (bottom), 43, 47, 52, 70, 76, 89, 122, and 130: © 1999 Harvey Helfand
page 148: © David Rubin, The Olin Partnership
page 159: © Bobrow Thomas Associates
pages 163, 164, 166 top, 168 bottom, 171 top, 172, 174 bottom, 175: © The SWA Group
page 165: © Robert Canfield, photographer
page 166 bottom: © David Wakely, photographer
page 167: © Rob Quigley Architects
page 168 top: © Peter Walker and Partners
page 169: © Tim Griffith, photographer
page 170: © Ellenzweig Associates
page 171 bottom: © Peter Aaron/ESTO
page 173: © Jay Graham, photographer
page 174 bottom: © Brent Martin, MBT Architecture

LIBRARY OF CONGRESS CATALOGUING-IN-PUBLICATION DATA
Joncas, Richard, 1953–
  Stanford University / Richard Joncas, David J. Neuman, and Paul V. Turner.— 2nd ed.
    p. cm. — (The campus guide)
  Includes bibliographical references and index.
  ISBN 1-56898-538-X (alk. paper)
  1. Stanford University—Guidebooks. 2. Stanford University—Buildings. 3. Stanford University—
Buildings—Pictorial works. 4. Stanford University—History. I. Neuman, David J. II. Turner,
Paul Venable. III. Title. IV. Campus guide (New York, N.Y.)
  LD3031.J65 2006
  378.794'73—dc22
                                                                    2005021313

CONTENTS

How to use this book

This guide is intended for visitors, alumni, and students who wish to have an insider's look at the most historic and interesting buildings on campus, from the Main Quad by Shepley Rutan, and Coolidge, to the Allen Center for Integrated Systems by Antoine Predock and the Center for Clinical Sciences Research by Norman Foster.

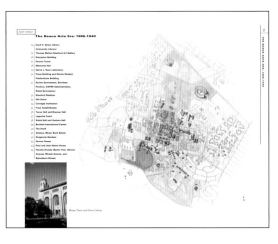

The book is divided into seven Parts; each covers a specific period of building across the entire campus. Each Part, or section, contains an introduction followed by a list of buildings (or cluster of buildings), illustrated on a three-dimensional map, with entries of historical and architectural information and photographs.

Campus buildings open: 9AM–5PM Monday–Friday; closed holidays.
Grounds open: dawn–dusk daily, year-round.
Walking tours: 11:00AM and 3:15PM Monday–Friday; year-round except holidays. Admission: free, start at Visitor Information Services.
Driving tours: 1:00PM Monday–Friday; year-round except during finals and holidays. Admission: $5; reservations recommended, start at Visitor Information Services.
Hoover Tower observation deck open: 10:00AM–4:30PM daily. Admission: $2 adults; $1 seniors and children; free Stanford faculty, staff, and students.
Iris & B. Gerald Cantor Center for Visual Arts: 11AM–5PM Wednesday–Sunday; 11AM–8 PM Thursday; closed holidays. Admission: free

Further Information from:
Stanford University
Visitor Information Services
Memorial Auditorium, Memorial Hall
Stanford, CA 94305
650.723.2560
www.stanford.edu

Foreword

During the almost thousand-year history of universities, campuses have always been physical spaces. As we end the twentieth century, some university interactions have moved to cyberspace and the level of activity there grows at a breathtaking speed. At this stage of development, however, the university is still localized in time and space. The university as a place has found its most striking expression in the Anglo-Saxon world. Oxford, Cambridge, Harvard, William and Mary, Yale, Princeton, Virginia, and Stanford are all physical places, campuses to which students remove themselves for a number of years. They are also places students feel connected with for the rest of their lives.

For alumni, memories of their colleges or universities clearly include the physical setting and the architecture or architectures that make up the campuses. I am not aware of "exit interviews" that ask graduating seniors about "environmental influences" on their education in anything other than a metaphorical sense. On the other hand, students and alumni returning to their alma mater frequently display a feeling of "homecoming" that parallels what may be experienced on a return visit to one's hometown: famous landmarks and cozy corners trigger associations that are historical, aesthetic, personal.

Sometime ago, in a circle of friends who had attended or were attending a variety of colleges and universities, I asked those present what they associated with the architecture of their campus. They responded by talking about how *their* college represented the "quintessential" college to them: the architecture created community; the architecture connected them to history and tradition; commons, quads, and plazas constituted public fora; eighteenth-century buildings with their simple lines were recalled but also the beauty of recent, modern additions were praised; even the attribute "majestic" was invoked; quirky, unusual, and bizarre architecture figured in the recollections; much emphasis was placed on natural surroundings.

One of those present was a Stanford alumna who was born and raised on the East Coast and who had graduated some thirty years ago. She described her reaction to the Stanford campus as she approached it coming up Palm Drive: "I was stunned. The Spanish architecture was outside my experience. The Main Quad and the foothills behind it were physically different from anything that I had thought of in relation to college. At first, I was not sure I liked it."

Her direct and vivid reaction was admirably refreshing. The complex that is made up of the Outer Quad, Memorial Court, and the Inner Quad, and which is characterized by its Beaux Arts approach, Romanesque design, and the vast expanse of the California Missions style courtyard, with

Main Quad; Memorial Church in background

its arcades and Memorial Church, constitutes an ensemble whose effect is unique in American campus architecture.

The adaptation by Henry Hobson Richardson and Charles A. Coolidge of Romanesque features and arabesque stone carvings connect the yellow sandstone arches and cloisters to the California missions of the eighteenth century, as Leland Stanford wanted, to Mexico and Spain, and through Spain to the classical architecture of Rome and Greece. The language is powerful and poses the great challenge of how to design and build a century later.

The world often forgets that the visual art we are most exposed to on a daily basis is architecture: architecture pure and simple and architecture in its sculptural potential. It has the wonderful, but also frequently distressing, quality of being inescapable. This is why competitive architectural design is so important in the exercise of good stewardship at our universities—maintaining the physical endowment that has been handed down to us and, then, renewing it as needed to meet the changing nature of teaching, learning, and research, but also of aesthetics. While the Latin proverb says there is no disputing about taste, the Latin proverb is wrong. Aesthetics are an appropriate subject for debate, especially on campuses. It would be sad indeed if we did not strive for beauty (and the dignity that our founders hoped for) in a contemporary vocabulary. Stanford University has not always been successful in that pursuit but it is what the University has definitely attempted to do in the last decade of the century.

In the circle of those with whom I talked about the campus environment was a then current Stanford student. She said: "It is a gift to be on the Stanford campus. If you do not enjoy some part of it every day, you feel guilty for rejecting a gift." I hope this book will give its readers and users a sense of that gift. It is the second edition of a campus guide first published in 1999. At that time, a number of major buildings were still under construction. Others have been added since.

Stanford's additions continue to support its leadership in teaching, learning, and research on the one hand, and in athletics on the other. Together, they support the successful Campaign for Undergraduate Education, a one billion dollar fundraising effort dedicated exclusively to our undergraduates. This gift from Stanford's alumni and friends was the inspiration for this second edition of the *Stanford Campus Guide.*

Gerhard Casper
President Emeritus
Stanford University

The Stanford Campus: Its Place in History

Paul V. Turner

In 1886, Leland and Jane Stanford, planning the university that was to commemorate their recently deceased only child, chose the two most renowned designers in America to create the campus at their vast estate south of San Francisco. These were Frederick Law Olmsted, the pioneering landscape planner, and the preeminent architect Henry Hobson Richardson, whose young associate Charles Coolidge assumed the commission when Richardson died that year.

The Stanfords, however, had their own strong vision of the campus. And Leland Stanford was used to being in charge of big projects, having planned the western portion of the transcontinental railroad, and having served as governor of and then U.S. senator from California. The ensuing collaboration between architects and clients, to design the new campus, was frustrating especially to Olmsted, whose ideas were often overruled by Senator Stanford. But despite this difficult design process, the resulting master plan for the university, established in 1888, was powerful and innovative. And in several ways it was a turning point in American campus design.

Master plan of Stanford, by Frederick Law Olmsted and Charles Coolidge, 1888

The *campus*—a term first applied to college grounds at Princeton in the eighteenth century—is a distinctively American phenomenon, which began developing in colonial New England and Virginia. Typically set apart from cities, it is a kind of utopian community, self-sufficient and cohesive, but extroverted rather than cloistered, looking confidently to the outside world. The Stanford campus epitomizes this tradition in its rural location (at least originally rural), its integration of academic facilities and student housing, and its attention to open space and landscaping.

But the master plan for Stanford, as seen in a bird's-eye perspective rendering of 1888, was more ambitious and monumental than any previous campus design. Approached from the mile-long Palm Drive, the buildings of the Quad are organized around two axes: the major north-south axis, which leads through Memorial Court to the Inner Quad and focuses on Memorial

Church; and a secondary east-west axis, which originally was to extend from the Inner Quad into additional quadrangles as the university grew.

The monumental scale and clarity of this concept were due mainly to the Stanfords. Olmsted's first proposal, sketched when he visited the Palo Alto estate in September of 1886, was for a relatively modest arrangement of buildings set in the hills to the south of the present Quad. But Leland Stanford insisted on a flat site that would allow a more formal composition. And as the design evolved in 1887, in a give-and-take among Olmsted, Coolidge, and the Stanfords (Olmsted back in Boston, and Coolidge traveling from coast to coast), the design became increasingly monumental.

The architects prevailed on some points, as when Olmsted convinced the clients that Mediterranean landscaping was more appropriate than English-style lawns. But the basic character of the plan was determined mainly by the Stanfords, as suggested in an on-site report Coolidge sent to Olmsted in May of 1887:

> We had the surveyors stake out [the buildings], and when it was completed we went over the ground with [the Stanfords] and they said it faced to wrong way. . . . They also desired a vista up and down the valley thro' the side quadrangles and finally we told them that this would change the grade and upset your work to which the Gov. replied a Landscape Arch't and an Arch't might be disappointed but he was going to have the buildings the way he wanted them.

The great scale of the master plan may reflect Leland Stanford's railroad-building experience. (In fact, the sequence of aligned quadrangles suggests the forthright linearity of a railroad track or train.) But the monumentality of the design was due mainly to the memorial motive of the university. To Leland and Jane Stanford, only the most splendid undertaking would commemorate properly their lost child.

Perspective rendering of design for Stanford buildings, 1888

*Frederick Law Olmsted's
first plan for Stanford,
September 1886*

In the larger picture of American architecture, these traits of grandeur and formality happened to be appropriate also to a new type of American university that was appearing at the end of the nineteenth century: large, complex institutions concerned with public image and future growth. These traits can be seen, for example, in the master plans of Columbia University in New York of 1894, the University of California at Berkeley of 1899, and the universities of Wisconsin and Minnesota of 1908–1910. The Stanford master plan also reflected the Beaux Arts principles of the emerging City Beautiful movement in America, with its visions of great boulevards, plazas, and inspiring public buildings. Thus, for reasons unrelated to the Stanfords' personal motives, their university became a model for the ambitious campus plans of many American institutions in the early twentieth century.

The buildings themselves that enclose the Quad are often called Spanish or Mission Style, but a more correct designation is Richardsonian Romanesque—the style created in the 1870s and 1880s by H. H. Richardson, using forms from medieval Romanesque churches of France and Spain, interpreted to create impressions of solidity, strength, the honest use of materials, and a bold contrast between unadorned surfaces and richly decorated details. The Stanford buildings were Charles Coolidge's first commission following the death of his teacher, and he worked faithfully in Richardson's manner.

*Rendering design for Inner Quad arcade,
circa 1888*

Most remarkable is the way the individual buildings of the Quad—the church, the one-story classroom buildings of the Inner Quad, and the higher multipurpose structures of the Outer Quad—are linked by a complex system of arcades. These not only serve the practical functions of protection from rain, shading of classroom windows, and organization of pedestrian circulation; they unify the entire complex visually and make it more than the sum of its individual buildings. This pattern of arcaded linkage, more typical of European public spaces than American ones, is probably the most important feature of the original Stanford architecture.

The arcades that ring the Inner Quad are also the main reason that this space is reminiscent of the Spanish missions of old California. The association was apparently in Leland Stanford's mind from the earliest days of the project, when he said he wanted the university to be distinctively Californian. In fact, the Stanford Quad was the first major architectural design alluding to California missions, and it inaugurated the Mission Revival style that became pervasive in the American West in the following decades.

Leland Stanford Junior Museum, 1891

Long-range master plans for campuses are notoriously ineffective. They are usually doomed by new architectural fashions, changing educational needs, financial considerations, or the desire of individual donors for new buildings that stand out from the rest. At Stanford, the founders were able to execute enough of their vision that the essence of the master plan has endured. But departure from the plan began soon after Leland Stanford's death in 1893, when Jane Stanford took charge of the institution. Struggling with financial and legal difficulties, she succeeded in completing the Quad buildings and in keeping the university afloat, but she also demonstrated her independence by constructing additional buildings along Palm Drive, most with classical styles very different from that of the Quad.

Two of these Palm Drive buildings, a gymnasium and a library, were destroyed by the earthquake of 1906, but the Chemistry Building and the central part of the Stanford Museum survive—the latter being architecturally important as one of the first public buildings in the world constructed of reinforced concrete. Other university buildings damaged in the 1906 earthquake were repaired, although the massive Memorial Arch and the tower of Memorial Church were never rebuilt.

Memorial Arch and Memorial Church tower, before 1906

In the 1910s and 1920s, as the university grew and additional buildings were needed, new patterns of planning replaced the axial clarity of the original master plan. The San Francisco architectural firm of Bakewell and Brown designed most of the new buildings, including the university library, the student union, men's and women's gymnasiums, and several dormitories. Most of these structures were located relatively far from the Quad—to the south, east, and west—signaling that the campus would henceforth develop around several centers rather than one focal point.

Bakewell and Brown developed a plan for a Library Quad to the east of the main Quad, but rather than being open along the east-west axis as envisioned in the original plan, the new quad had the library on this axis, creating a more complex pattern of buildings and circulation. And as this part of the campus developed, with the library, the Education Building, the Art Gallery, Hoover Tower, and Memorial Auditorium, the notion of a quadrangle was lost altogether, replaced by a more traditional pattern of individual buildings fronting on streets. Most individual of all was the 285-foot-tall Hoover Tower, today still the only strongly vertical form on the horizontally scaled campus.

Despite their novel locations and shapes, these buildings by Bakewell and Brown used styles that reflected in varying ways the architecture of the Quad buildings. Typically they simplified the forms of the Quad, and sandstone was replaced by concrete or other materials, but arches, decorative motifs, and the proportions of the buildings made overt references to the Quad.

This architectural continuity was broken after World War II, when campus architect Eldridge T. Spencer produced several flat-roofed structures in a forthrightly "modern" style. The most prominent of these, the Stern Hall dormitory complex, provoked an indignant outcry from alumni, resulting in a university policy that required new buildings to have red-tile roofs and other superficial similarities to the Quad architecture, such as sandstone-like color. This policy was largely in force from the 1960s through the 1980s, at least in the central campus area. As a result, most of the buildings from this period have a loose uniformity—what might be called a Red-Tile Roof Style—despite their differences in size, shape, and materials. Examples are Meyer Library, the Cummings Art Building, the business school, and the law school. The most notable exception is the complex of medical school buildings designed in 1959 by Edward Durell Stone, in a style inspired by the "textile-block" designs of Frank Lloyd Wright late in his career.

The post-World War II decades at Stanford saw an explosion in automotive traffic, as at most universities. This led to the decision, about 1950, to create a ring road—Campus Drive—within which traffic was limited in various ways, especially in the central zone around the Quad. But proliferating parking lots became an increasing factor in the university's land use planning, vying with proposed new buildings for the dwindling open space on campus. Despite Stanford's large land endowment—over eight thousand acres—only a relatively small part of the property is practically available for university facilities, so the constant pressure to construct new facilities is in conflict with preservation of the central open spaces that were an essential component of the original master plan.

In recent years the main focus of university construction has been in the Near West Campus, the area to the west of the Quad, devoted largely to science and engineering. Many of the existing structures there were temporary or haphazardly sited, and in the 1980s master plans were developed for the area. As new buildings have been designed for it, the previous red-tile formula has given way to greater latitude in architectural style, and prestigious architects have been invited to make more personal design interpretations of the Stanford theme—as in Antoine Predock's CIS Extension, James Freed's Science and Engineering Quad, Ricardo Legorreta's Schwab Residential Center, and Robert Stern's Gates Building. Ironically, despite the greater freedom, some of the new buildings, especially Gates Hall, make more literal reference to the Richardsonian Romanesque Quad than did anything from the red-tile era, reflecting postmodern interest in historical styles.

Moreover, the new Science and Engineering Quad attempts to recover something of the spatial organization of the original Olmsted-Stanford plan. The buildings are arranged to form a kind of quadrangle, along the east-west axis formed by the Main Quad, and the importance given to this concept was emphasized by the demolition, in 1997, of a physics lecture hall that had been erected in the 1950s, to allow an unimpeded view along this axis from the Quad to the west.

A renewed appreciation of the original architecture of Stanford is also seen in the attention given in recent years to the Quad itself: the paving of the Inner Quad, as intended by Olmsted; the extensive seismic upgrading of the Quad buildings, beginning with History Corner in 1979; and the historical sensitivity epitomized by the 1997 restoration of Building 30 to its original condition.

There has recently been increased awareness, in the Stanford community, of the historic value of its campus—not only in the buildings of the Quad, but also in the underlying principles of the original master plan and its open spaces. Along with the University of Virginia, designed by Thomas Jefferson in 1817, Stanford presents probably the best example in America of a powerful master plan that was largely executed, has been conscientiously preserved, and serves as the continuing inspiration for future development.

The Stanford Campus: Into Its Second Century

David J. Neuman

As Stanford University approached its centennial in 1991, much thought was given to both its history and its future. This internal assessment included the evaluation of its original master plan by Frederick Law Olmsted and Leland and Jane Stanford; and its prospective rejuvenation in order to reestablish a sense of unity and harmony that had been lost during several epochs of subsequent building development, each with its own sense of campus planning and related purpose. These development eras range from the Beaux Arts eclecticism of the latter days of Jane Stanford and the extended period of Bakewell and Brown to the later modernism of Church, Warnecke, and Spencer. Each had left its distinctive, yet mostly unrelated, impression on the original order of the campus. Yet such was the power of the original plan, with its strong axial arrangement, emphasizing the relationship of its architecture, landscape, and natural setting, that its intent was still evident to both the casual user and the interested professional, despite its diminished form one hundred years later.

The plan's basic tenets of connectivity, balance and order, were carefully studied within the context of the predicted demands for education and research into the university's next century. The outcome was the confirmation that the founding principles of Stanford's campus plan remained solid and relevant; therefore, the original plan that so clearly represented these intentions could serve as the basis for future redevelopment and/or expansion.

The Leland Stanford Junior University, General Plan, 1888

With further clarification, the plan could again be the visible manifestation of Stanford's continuing commitment to reason and beauty, to order and complexity, to history and opportunity. These physical planning guidelines tenets were assembled in a graphic report and presented to the Stanford Board of Trustees in May 1991, as "The Plan for the Second Century"; and were received enthusiastically.

As an important part of this planning renaissance, the hierarchy of plan (order), landscape (natural setting), and architecture (facility) was reestablished in keeping with the Olmsted-Stanford plan. In contrast to the environments of earlier American campuses, like Yale University with its

SECOND CENTURY PLANNING PRINCIPLES

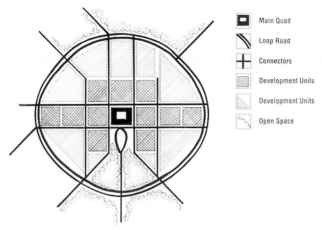

▣	Main Quad
◥	Loop Road
✚	Connectors
▦	Development Units
◺	Development Units
⬟	Open Space

Second Century Planning Principles

village green and the University of Virginia with its central lawn, each of which was mostly defined by its architectural surroundings, Stanford's campus environment is set by the order of the plan and the landscape environment, both natural and manmade, with its architecture set clearly in this context. A set of "fundamental elements" recognized firmly the prominence of the axes, loop road, and Mediterranean landscape, along with the Main Quadrangle and the flanking linear quad organization. In addition, a hierarchy of planning from broad land use plans to individual site plans was recognized and the need for design guidelines in all major regions—such as core campus, medical center, and residential areas—was clearly affirmed. These concepts, when coupled with the stated goals to "preserve and restore historic and environmental features" and to "enhance the visual character" of the campus, have set the groundwork for the character of the planning and campus design activities that have successfully followed. Initial examples include the Main Quad Design Guidelines (Office of the University Architect, with Hardy, Holzman, Pfeiffer, 1991, revised 1995), which has guided the seismic repairs, restoration, and infrastructure upgrade of the twenty-six buildings comprising the Stanford Main Quad (1990–99); and the Palm Drive restoration project (1992), which not only repaired the quality of the street, sidewalks, and landscape, but also finally developed the granite-curbed, entryway as intended in Frederick Law Olmsted's unfinished design. Both projects have been enthusiastically received, earning several design awards, including those from the American Society of Landscape Architects (ASLA) in 1994 and the American Institute of Architects (AIA) in 1998.

Additional design guidelines for the central campus and the medical center were separately developed so that they recognized not only the

Palm Drive (1992)

programmatic and architectural diversity of each region, but also the site planning and landscape similarities. These guidelines reestablish the site planning principles of vista, circulation, and connectivity in such a fashion as to mandate the restoration of the grandeur of the original plan without necessitating wholesale demolition of poorly sited buildings. Instead, they call for careful accommodation of landscape patterns and materials; and set various building design controls, especially in massing and material options. In short, requiring new facilities, both architecture and landscape, to be *of* Stanford, not merely *at* Stanford, as had happened so often in the past. The hierarchy of plan, landscape and architecture is thus reinforced on a project-by-project basis. To fill in the gaps among the individual project sites, an aggressive program of landscape connectivity projects ranging from pedestrian walks and bikeways to site furnishings, lighting, and signage was developed under the Stanford Infrastructure Program (sip). Funded by a surcharge on capital projects, it has supported projects that significantly enhance the harmony and functionality of both campus and medical center within the past decade. A prime example of such a project is Serra Mall, the major east-west circulation element across the campus. Once a collection of marginally controlled, auto-dominant street sections and parking areas, it has become a narrowed bicycle and shuttle bus way with separated sidewalks. Along its route, more

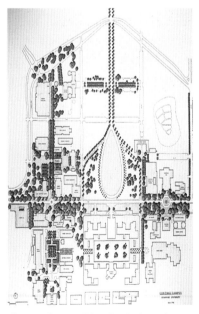

Central Campus Plan for the Second Century (1997)

than two acres of formerly paved area has been returned to landscaped open space. It is being used as a model for the renovation of both Lasuen and Lomita Malls, also former streets, which run on either side of the Main Quad. Together with Palm Drive, these three malls are the pedestrian and bicycle arteries of the campus core.

Though more than two-thirds of Stanford's billion dollar capital development program over the past decade has been devoted to replacement or restoration of existing space, substantial new buildings have been added to the campus. As mentioned previously, each has been subject to rigorous design guidelines with regard to siting, massing, architectural character,

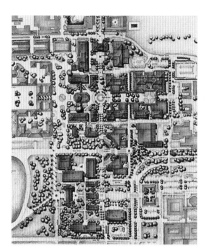

Near West Campus Plan, The Architects Collaborative (1986–1987)

Detail of Science and Engineering Quad

and material palette. In short, each has been a carefully inserted infill project, in which each contributes to the whole of the campus. The best example to cite is also the largest of these, the $120 million Science and Engineering Quad (SEQ). Although the current plan is sometimes attributed to the 1986–87 Near West Campus Plan by The Architects Collaborative (TAC), it is actually a direct development of the Olmsted-Stanford plan and the Plan for the Second Century in its reliance on the axial ordering set by Serra Mall and the Main Quad's east-west axis and its use of perimeter arcades to define the central space. The design by James Ingo Freed and Laurie Olin was chosen through an invited design competition in 1995. (Since Gerhard Casper became president of Stanford in 1992, all major architectural commissions have been the subject of design competitions following his direction and reflecting his determination to attain excellence in each project's design.) Freed supports the notion of historically and contextually motivating factors when he states, "Our first task was to establish where you are and where you are going." Olin adds that the SEQ, like the Main Quad of Stanford's original plan, creates an "order that could extend off indefinitely," an order which architectural critic Aaron Betsky surmises will "tie the campus to its physical and symbolic roots." In this fashion, the four new SEQ buildings, which replace four others of modest architectural merit, are contemporary variations on the Stanford theme, that is, of this special place. Betsky notes the following:

> The McCullough Materials Laboratory Annex and the Statistics Department Building are closest to the campus core. Their design tries to adapt the bearing-wall and gable-roof construction you find there to a modern idiom.... the Electrical Engineering Department Building and the Regional Teaching facility then start to break open and abstract these forms into larger, geometric masses and expressive curves ... that gesture towards the new part of the campus. (*Architectural Record*, July 1996)

Center for Clinical Sciences Research, Foster and Partners (1997–2000)

Other projects, ranging from Ricardo Legorreta's Schwab Residential Learning Center on the east side of the core campus, to Antoine Predock's Allen Center for Integrated Systems on the west side, and Norman Foster's Center for Clinical Sciences Research at the medical center, follow the same integrating approach to complex and competing challenges: site/landscape/architecture and historic context/current program. Each is successful because of its resolution of these issues and response to a specific context and guidelines. President Casper issued the following challenge to me as University Architect, and to all of Stanford's planners and designers: "By the turn of the century, I hope that Stanford will have a campus second to none, not only in its beauty, but also its functionality." The work completed in the current epoch is responding well to that challenge, as architectural author and critic Michael Cannell wrote in 1997:

> As they pass among flower beds and arches, sunlit tiles and shaded arcades, students will see that the smallest details help to express the whole. As a place restored, Stanford can be an example to those who would look beyond the ubiquitous influence of cars and other small-scale conveniences. The Stanford of this twenty-first century might not be perfect, but it does suggest that all the glories of nineteenth-century landscape design can live again. And that is an exciting prospect.

Introduction to the Guide

Richard Joncas

Throughout its history, Stanford University has struggled to mediate its past and present architecture, landscape, and planning. This historical dialogue reveals itself in distinct geographical and chronological zones that define the campus plan. Lauded by Lewis Mumford for its "concentration, compactness, [and] unity," the heart of the campus, known as the inner and outer quads, has affected all subsequent building on campus and has been both its great strength and its bane. Each architectural generation, whether Richardsonian Romanesque, Beaux-Arts, the international style, brutalism, or postmodernism, has endeavored to marry its idiosyncratic style with the original buildings and landscape. Following Frederick Law Olmsted's proposals, later quads were sited loosely along the cross axis, although none were fully realized, resulting in a casual dispersal of buildings around a tightly ordered center. Nevertheless, periodic building campaigns organized around the concept of quads developed sharply demarcated areas of the campus, each leaving its own historical imprint. Recent events, including the 1989 Loma Prieta earthquake, moreover, have prompted an era of restoration and renewal, and reinforcement of the planning ideals embodied in Olmsted's quad plan.

The history of Stanford architecture is inseparable from issues of landscaping and the confrontation between the campus's rural and urban identities. This conflict has distinguished the work of the preeminent landscape architects who have shaped the university's lands, beginning with Olmsted in the 1880s; Gardner Dailey in the 1920s; Thomas Church, Robert Royston, and Laurence Halprin after World War II; and more recently George Hargreaves, Laurie Olin, and Peter Walker, among others. Each has left his stamp, inspired by the original plan and the distinctive beauty of California's foothills, fields, and climate. Olmsted set the tone, forging an extensive, yet unified, campus out of a rich mix of virgin lands, planted wilderness regions and monumental axes, and drives and courts calculated to enhance the native spirit of the sandstone architecture. The variety of Stanford's landscapes underscores a regionalism devoted to distinct academic, aesthetic, and social purposes: to foster an interdisciplinary exchange of ideas; to mitigate visually the impact of buildings; and ultimately, to nurture the sense of a single community of distinct parts.

The guide is a history of this campus's architecture, landscape, and planning, which are inevitably the consequence of shifting academic priorities and needs generated by the university's continuous, and sometimes phenomenal growth and development. In this book we present that history as it unfolds chronologically and geographically, with each Walk providing an overview of the significant issues and events characterizing a given period, followed by a discussion of the most important buildings and spaces.

PART ONE

The Stanford Farm and

Other Early Buildings

1

Stanford Farm

N

The Stanford Farm and Other Early Buildings

In 1876 Leland Stanford began acquiring land in the Santa Clara Valley for a country haven and stock farm. This isolated, idyllic region of the mid-peninsula, some thirty miles south of San Francisco, became the unlikely setting for the Leland Stanford Junior University. The railroad magnate, who had been governor of California in the 1860s and became a U. S. senator in early 1885, had amassed over 4,000 acres by 1882 for his experimental horse farm (one of the largest in the world), where he indulged his passion for breeding champion trotters and, later, other thoroughbred racing stock. Additional parcels purchased would put the total acreage of the Stock Farm at over 8,400 by 1892. Stanford's innovative breeding and training practices were evident in the farm's organization, which had importance for the design of Stanford University: at its heart was an "immense quadrangle," as the press described it, of barns, stables, outbuildings, and dwellings. Colts were placed in a "kindergarten," a miniature track where they were trained by one of the most prominent horsemen, or "professors," of the day, Charles Marvin, who superintended the farm. Studs were stabled by their different classes, each receiving its own building, enclosure, and manager. These features, including the farm itself, later became prominent characteristics of the university. The site is also important for the development of Eadweard Muybridge's motion-study photographs of horses, the technology which Stanford helped invent in an effort to improve the training of his horses. Portions of the original site remain, notably along the western edge of the main campus around the Red Barn.

1. Stanford Estate

1863; addition, 1888; partially destroyed, 1906; demolished, 1966

Stanford Mansion

The original house was Mayfield Grange, which Stanford purchased in 1876. In 1888 a three-story central block was added. The Italianate style house sat in the center of several hundred acres (once part of Rancho San Francisquito), informally land-scaped in the picturesque conventions of the day, which the house echoed in its irregular massing and silhouette and porch wrapped along its southern face (the original Gordon house). There is the intimation of Gothic inspiration in its accretion of recessed and projecting boxes. The later center block was crowned by a high Second

Empire style roof and dormer characteristic of the curious hybrids being fashioned in the Pacific west during the 1880s. The juxtaposition of the formal and picturesque would later dominate the planning of the Stanford campus.

2. Palo Alto Stock Farm

Stock Farm *1876 following*
Red Barn *1878–1879*

Leland Stanford's 8,400-acre Stock Farm

The Stock Farm and its vast holdings, including pastures, racetracks, paddocks, and stables, were named after the local natural landmark, El Palo Alto, an especially tall redwood tree. The Red Barn sat at the center of Stanford's horse farm, where some 600 horses were boarded. It is one of the few surviving examples of Victorian barn architecture: an elegant, if utilitarian structure with distinctive Eastlake-like stick style elements in the high, pointed gables on the front and sides. The barn continues to be used today, following its restoration and modernization in 1984 by Esherick Homsey Dodge and Davis of San Francisco.

Palo Alto Stock Farm

3. Lake Lagunita *1878*

Lake Lagunita

Lake Lag, as it is usually called, served as a reservoir for the Stock Farm, which included orchards and alfalfa fields. The lake was created by damming Los Trancos Creek and pumping in seasonal waters. The porous nature of the ground, however, required Leland Stanford to line the lake bed with tons of clay, which was tamped down by sheep. The clay never proved successful in holding the seasonal waters, and reportedly, over the years much of it was dug up for flowerbeds in the faculty housing areas.

4. Peter Coutts's Ayershire Farm *1875–1882*

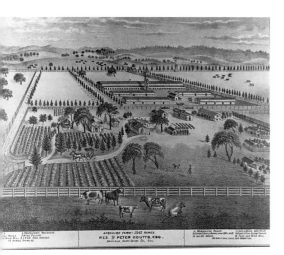

Peter Coutts's Farm

Jean Baptiste Paulin Caperon (1822–1889), who adopted the pseudonym of Peter Coutts, is one of Stanford's more colorful and mysterious characters. A Swiss-born Parisian banker, Coutts purchased 1,400 acres in 1875–76, the center of which is the current Escondido Village. Coutts raised championship livestock, and the site originally contained fifteen wood buildings, including barns, stables, a clock tower, and a brick dairy house supporting his industry. The property was called Matadero Ranch, after the creek that passed through it, though it was popularly known as Ayershire Farm after Coutts's famous cattle. Coutts returned to France when events threatened his fortune. Failing health kept him abroad, and in 1882 he sold his farm to Leland Stanford.

Escondite Cottage Coutts built a simple cottage for himself, his two children, and their governess (it was called Escondite, or "hidden," Cottage), as a temporary home until plans were ready for a large (never built) chateau on the crest of Pine Hill. The house was known for its chintz wallpaper and odd French furniture. A second story was added after Coutts left for France. Charles Coolidge resided in the cottage during the design of the Inner Quad. David Starr Jordan, the university's first president, lived in the house between 1891 and 1893. The house serves currently as the

Escondite Cottage

Tower House

administrative offices for Escondido Village, a graduate student housing area.

Frenchman's Study (Tower House) Coutts built a separate study for himself that was rumored to contain rare books. Once crowned by a tall Second Empire roof, it is now truncated, with the woodframe and brick house the sole remnant of a once extensive holding. Damaged in the 1989 Loma Prieta earthquake, it was closed at that time and awaits repair and renovation.

Frenchman's Reservoir The reservoir, or lake, no longer exists, but some of the boulders forming the bridge and other ruins that occupied the site during the 1870s remain. The reservoir was part of Coutts's plan to build a chateau on Pine Hill that would be approached along a tree-lined drive and an artificial lake. The lake featured a bridge and a small island occupied by a ruined cottage. The reservoir, at one time used as a dump by the university for 1906 earthquake debris, was drained in 1922 as a health hazard. Across the way on the hill is Frank Lloyd Wright's Hanna-Honeycomb House (1936), and below it, at the base of the hill, is a cave (presently sealed), which was excavated by Coutts in his search for a water supply.

Frenchman's Tower On the southern boundary of his property, Coutts built a circular, crenelated tower inspired by the mid-nineteenth-century fad for romantic Gothic Revival ruins. It housed a water tank, according to one source, and is currently closed to any use.

Frenchman's Tower

PART TWO

The Original Campus: 1886–1906

*Stanford Campus with Lake Lagunita
before the 1906 earthquake*

14

10

11

8
7
9
5
6
17
18
16
15

13

18

19

21

21
22

À
N

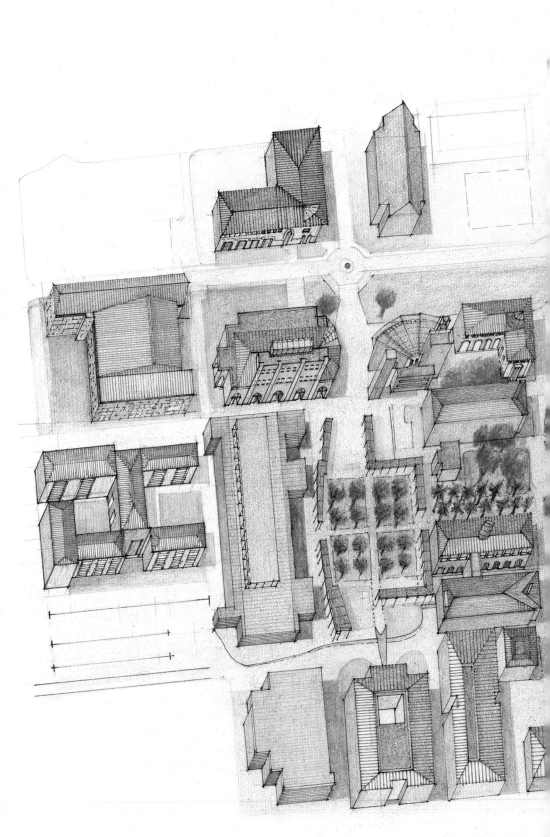

Main Quad: Inner Quad, Outer Quad

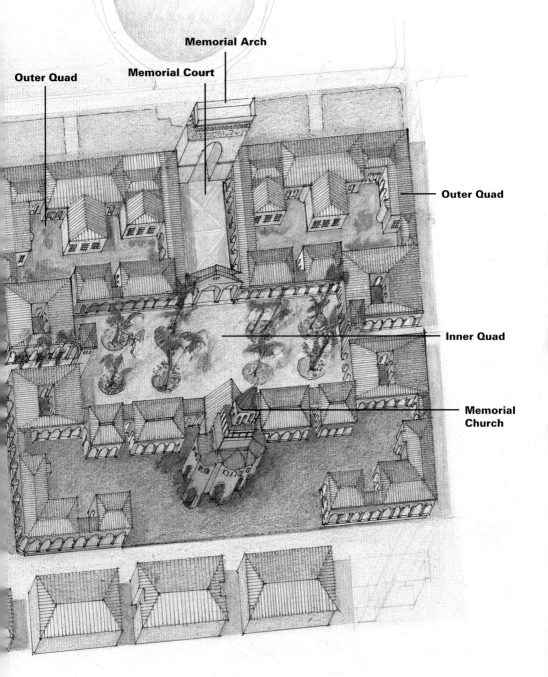

Outer Quad

Memorial Court

Memorial Arch

Outer Quad

Inner Quad

Memorial Church

Olmsted-Stanford Planning

Stanford University was born from tragedy. In 1884, as Leland and Jane Stanford were concluding a tour of Europe, their only child was stricken with typhoid and died in Florence. Heartbroken at the loss of their fifteen-year-old son, they devoted the remainder of their lives and their fortune to his memory. Their decision to found a university, as well as a museum, honored his (and their) enthusiasm for education, collecting, and the public welfare. Leland Stanford Junior University would become a "new engine of civilization," according to its founders. The technological metaphor was not happenstance: as one of the builders of the transcontinental railroad, Leland Stanford was identified with the technological spirit of progress in the West.

Stanford University, as it is now known, was to be a free institution, charging only room and board, and thereby offering an education to all social groups (tuition was first charged in 1920.) The university would train "useful" students in the mechanical arts and sciences, and these students would in turn bring about modern "labor-aiding machines," as Stanford called them, enhancing production and increasing prosperity for all. The university's educational mission, from the "kindergarten pupils to the post-graduate," Stanford declared, was the "physical and intellectual improvement of mankind," by which he meant the development of the soul. Stanford believed that a strictly technical education stifled the imagination, and that all great civilizations were characterized by a belief in the "Divine Creator" and the immortality of the soul. Education, he opined, was the humanizing influence of civilization.

Victorian America frequently conventionalized memory in grand public designs. At Stanford, this propensity is played out in the creation of a sequence of contained spaces punctuated by imposing monuments. The design of the university would reflect the Stanfords' belief in technological progress and religion. Their educational ground plan undergirded the design of the campus. Quadrangles, capable of continual extension along their major axes, permitted Stanford's "indefinite expansion" of intellectual knowledge. "We may always advance toward the infinite," Leland Stanford affirmed. With their organizing axes, the quads would bring order and civilization to the surrounding wilderness. The seemingly unlimited extent of grounds, held in trust by the university in perpetuity, was to become its outdoor laboratories, including the Stock Farm, with its own quadrangle of barns and kindergarten track, a true attempt at taming nature. Stanford would educate men and women "fit . . . to realize the possibilities of humanity, in order that our graduates may in a measure become missionaries to spread the correct ideas of civilization." Reinforcing this connection between the university and its pedagogic aspirations, Stanford adopted the architectural style of the California missions, which he promoted as an indigenous response to California's climate and landscape as one of the earliest instances of its revival. Stanford also wanted a harmonious composition of buildings, eschewing the eclectic, stylistic potpourri he had seen in the eastern United States.

As noted in Paul Turner's essay, between 1886 and 1887, Stanford commissioned Olmsted to lay out the campus and its grounds, and the firm of Shepley, Rutan, and Coolidge to design the buildings. Olmsted quipped that Stanford wanted a "Universitatory. . . . There is not any word big enough for his ideas of what it is to be." Stanford had already decided to adopt the parallelogram as the organizing principle of the university's campus before he hired his architects. The major north-south axis, aligned fifteen degrees east of north, terminated in the foothills south of the campus in a cemetery area known as the Knoll, where Stanford planned to erect the family's elegant mausoleum, popularized in the press as one of the grandest in the United States. However, as the plans evolved, and perhaps because of its distance and isolation, the mausoleum site was shifted, in one case north of the campus, directly opposite the church, in what was to be a new cemetery in Olmsted's arboretum. This plan, however, would have denied Stanford his grand approach, and the mausoleum was removed from the main axis, which became Palm Drive, and embowered much less conspicuously on a spot once intended for the Stanfords' new house, the plans for which were abandoned after Leland Junior's death.

The university's buildings, according to Charles Coolidge, their designer, were "Mission Style with Romanesque details." The primarily single-story buildings' relative simplicity and spareness; their long, continuous arcades; their deep window reveals; and their red-tile roofs evoked the "Spanishness" of mission architecture. Stanford was credited in the press for this stylistic borrowing, although Coolidge later claimed responsibility. The Inner Quad itself recalled the enclosed, often large quadrangle next to the mission church, fitting the buildings easily into their site while taking advantage of the largely benign climate. The deep, cavernous arcades and their ground-hugging horizontality, as well as the use of local sandstone, helped give the architecture its indigenous effect.

The university opened in October 1891, with the Inner Quad nearly finished. There were few ancillary buildings: the men's and women's dorms, some ten faculty houses, and the boiler house. Andrew White, president of Cornell University, visiting the campus shortly after the completion of the Inner Quad, mused: "Evening after evening I walked through the cloisters of the great quadrangle, admiring the solidity, beauty, and admirable arrangement of the buildings, and enjoying their lovely surroundings and the whole charm of that California atmosphere."

Jane Stanford began construction of Memorial Church and the surrounding outer quad in 1898, five years after the death of her husband.

Her almost superhuman building campaign, described by University President David Starr Jordan as the "second stone age," largely completed the Outer Quad and several buildings immediately to its north flanking Palm Drive, including the surviving Chemistry Building. Jane Stanford's quirky sense of style undermined the architectural harmony established by her husband, and the buildings erected outside the quad violated the fundamental order of Olmsted's original plan, a harbinger of future events.

5. Inner Quad *Shepley, Rutan, and Coolidge, 1887–1891*

Inner Quad

The heart and soul of the university is the Inner Quad. The campus's earliest architecture, the Inner Quad is a kind of medieval cloister drawn out to Californian scale and conceived in relation to the human presence within a vast landscape. Against the panorama of foothills and mountains to the south and the wilderness planted to the north, the expansive sweep of the arcade dramatizes the unifying rhythm and order the great space brings to its site. The unbroken field of the broad, red-tiled roof surfaces further reinforces the continuities between landscape and architecture. Only the tall gates at the east and west ends, a gabled arch decorated with rosettes to the north, and Memorial Church in the center of the south arcade interrupt the skyline. Hardly visible behind the deeply shaded passageways of the arcades and nestled under the tiled roofs are the twelve single-story education buildings. Their interiors, however, were double-height spaces providing thermal insulation from the hot California summer sun and cool winter and nighttime temperatures.

The rough-faced ashlar sandstone of the arcade and buildings, and the finely striated column shafts set on plinths and decorated with capitals of almost child-like simplicity (the tongue-and-heart patterns are derived from Mont Saint-Michel), lend the architecture the massive, "enduring and substantial" quality called for by Leland Stanford. President White of Cornell, further opined upon his visit to the early campus that "the buildings, in simplicity, beauty, and fitness, far surpassed any others which had at that time been erected for university purposes in the United States; and I feel sure that when the entire plan is carried out, not even Oxford or Cambridge will have anything more beautiful."

Stanford took precautions to protect the buildings from earth-quakes: he set the original Inner Quad on broad, flaring foundations. This feature was later ignored by his successors in completing the Outer Quad and the buildings flanking Palm Drive—with disastrous consequences in 1906 and 1989. The arcades, paved with Codman's artificial stone, are broad passages providing a corridor of communication among the various departments, each of which was housed in its own building. Stanford initially planned to plant grass to cover the Inner Quad, as in Eastern institutions, but Olmsted persuaded him to adopt a planting scheme more Mediterranean in character, with planted islands and a paved surface consisting of large, rectangular, coarse blocks of artificial stone like those used in the arcades, though this latter feature was never carried out (an "ashphaltum" covering remained until 1985 when a decorative precast concrete surface was added).

6. Memorial Church

Charles Coolidge, 1887; Clinton Day, revisions and addition, 1899–1902; rebuilt 1911–1913; 1989–1992

The Stanfords wanted a nonsectarian church to stand at the center of the university. Set into the middle of the long southern range of the Inner Quad, the church became the focal point terminating the long axis from Palm Drive. (Prior to its construction, a small, temporary chapel, which also served as the university's first assembly hall, was housed in Building 100 of the Inner Quad.) It is an opulent example of high Victorian architecture with sumptuous materials and arts. Erected by Jane Stanford in memory of her late husband, the church was originally designed by Coolidge, who modeled it after Richardson's Trinity Church (1876) in Boston. A modest copy of that cruciform plan, Memorial Church's semicircular apses once ringed a large, turreted belfry supported by flying buttresses (an addition to Coolidge's design made by Day), though the tower was brought down in the 1906 earthquake and was never rebuilt. Andrew White, Jane Stanford's frequent advisor and lecturer at the university, recommended the addition of chimes, which were installed between 1901 and 1902.

Jane Stanford, who was deeply inspired by San Marco in Venice, embellished Coolidge's spare design with dense ornamentation and iconography, on the exterior and interior. According to a Stanford publication at the time, the church emulated the "glorious color" of the great cathedrals of Europe, particularly of Italy, and their decorative arts—sculpture, mosaic, fresco, and glass. Beginning with the arches along the quad, its most luxuriant, the main elevation of the church displays carved foliation and decorative patterns lightened by sculpted cherub heads along its base (a motif continued in mosaic on the interior, above the round-headed windows of the nave). Above, the broad gable was carpeted with mosaic around a large quatrefoil window flanked by a series of smaller round-headed windows, where Coolidge had proposed only the central stained-glass window, a recurrent Mission element.

The facade mosaic by Antonio Paoletti, a Venetian genre painter, depicted an indefinite biblical scene described in a December 1900 contract as *Christ Blessing the People*. Although the mural became popularly known as the *Sermon on the Mount,* scholars agree the mosaic does not represent that scene from the Book of Matthew. Following the 1906 quake the facade was rebuilt with a classical round-headed window that more grandly restates the smaller flanking, arcuated openings. The destroyed mosaic was replaced by Salviati and Company, who executed the original.

Memorial Church "Round Room" under construction

Inside, a dimly lit cavern of glowing mosaic surfaces (by Paoletti) and vibrant, stained-glass windows (by Frederick Lamb Studios) is roofed over by an exposed-timber ceiling reminiscent of Trinity Church. The floor descends toward the crossing, where the space swells into three semicircular apses, with those on either end having galleries supported on columns. Further suggestive of the church's early purpose as an assembly hall is the raised floor of the main apse, which also served as a dais for commencement ceremonies. (Jane Stanford felt that such secular activities were inappropriate and built an assembly hall of comparable scale in the Outer Quad for such events.) Freestanding sculptures of the twelve apostles by Bernieri and Company of Carrara, Italy once stood in front of the niches, but were destroyed when the tower collapsed in 1906. A round room was added to the back of the church in 1902 by Clinton Day. The church has been rebuilt and strengthened twice after suffering heavy damage in the 1906 and 1989 earthquakes.

Encircling the university's inner sanctum is the Outer Quad. The hallmark of Jane Stanford's major building campaign, it was erected in stages by several architects, including Henry Schulze, George Washington Percy and Frederick F. Hamilton, and Charles Hodges, the university's first unofficial resident architect, though it was built largely as Coolidge designed it. From Palm Drive, the Outer Quad looms before a panorama of sky and rolling foothills, a continuous cliff of massive sandstone buildings topped by Spanish tile roofs and accented along its base by a deep, continuous arcade. Subsequently the north elevation's originally two-story structures (the interiors have been converted to three) border Serra Mall, a major thoroughfare originally landscaped by Olmsted, and stand on a high, graduated terrace formed from earth removed from the sunken oval fronting the quads. Scaled to the monumental approach, the great breadth and formality of the Outer Quad is organized into wings consisting of a large, slightly projecting central mass flanked by two lesser elements on either side of a memorial arch (destroyed in the 1906 quake).

The larger structures initially served the university's social and communal functions, housing the library, assembly hall, and a natural history museum (The Leland Stanford Junior Museum was also planned for the Outer Quad but was built elsewhere; see below). The earliest buildings, the library and the assembly hall, which formed the eastern range, were designed by Percy and Hamilton using Ernest Ransome's patented reinforced-concrete system, one of the hallmarks of the firm (see Museum and Roble Hall below). At the second-story height of the center blocks were sculptures of renowned figures such as Alexander von Humboldt and Louis Agassiz, whom Stanford had known, representing the pedagogic aspirations of the university. The skylit assembly hall, with its little theater, was built for secular ceremonies and contained two greenrooms on either side of the stage in a room planned without any angles. The natural history building at the center of the west flank contained a two-story, skylit museum court ringed by balconies lined with exhibits and specimens.

Outer Quad

The great height of the north elevation, requiring a steep flights of stairs at each corner, gives way along the sides to arcaded, single-story structures that gradually settle below grade as the site rises to the south (the southwest corner actually cuts into a rise in the grade by several feet). The outer arcade is punctuated at the center of the east and west flanks by gates leading to the Inner Quad and remains incomplete along the south elevation following its partial collapse in the 1906 quake. The curved corners were once named after the departments that occupied them—geology, engineering, zoology, and history. The corners along the north elevation contain busts of Leland Stanford and his son, set within cartouches. A buffer of paved courtyards, initially designed for building expansion, separates the Inner and Outer Quads.

8. Memorial Arch

Shepley, Rutan, and Coolidge, 1889; Charles Hodges, revisions, 1899–1902; John Evans, frieze design, 1900–1902; Rupert Schmid, sculptor, 1900–1902; partly destroyed, 1906

Memorial Arch

At the head of Palm Drive, a one-hundred-foot-high memorial arch, a monumental sandstone portal whose scale prompted popular comparisons to Yosemite, marked the threshold into the university's Inner Quad. Originally designed by Coolidge after a memorial in Buffalo by Richardson, the arch was heightened by Hodges at Jane Stanford's request, and its broad footings, devised by Leland Stanford against earthquakes, were later omitted during construction, causing its collapse in 1906. The gate's massiveness, moreover, was only superficial: built of unreinforced brick faced with stone, the arch was a hollow shell containing stairways at either end leading to an observation deck behind the tall machicolations.

The arch was crowned by a colossal, sculpted frieze, twelve feet high, representing the "Progress of Civilization in America" (a program suggested by Leland Stanford and prepared by Augustus Saint-Gaudens though never carried out by him). Its allegorical and historical figures portrayed the most important developments in the New World, notably the advents of Christianity, agriculture, and mechanical technology, all of which were portrayed in a benign light. Culminating the historical procession was present-day America, represented by the Stanfords on horseback blazing the trail for the railroad, superintended by the genius of engineering. The frieze, sculpted by Schmid, who was best known for his fountain sculpture, *California,* in the Grand Court of the California Midwinter International Exposition (1894), was inspired by the Parthenon's Panathenaic frieze in Athens but was given a local stamp, using student portraits as models for the figures and horses chosen from the Stanford stables. The frieze broadcasts the university's missionary quest to spread the humanizing gospel of practical and useful education coupled with a belief in Divine Providence. Only part of each base currently remains following the 1906 earthquake.

9. Memorial Court *Shepley, Rutan, and Coolidge, 1900*

Memorial Court

Memorial Court is a green space bridging the Inner and Outer Quads. It is largely the creation of Jane Stanford, who appropriated it to commemorate those who had died in the service of the university. Stanford rejected Olmsted's recommendation to pave the court, as in the Inner Quad, and instead ordered turf and paved walks centered on a sculpture group by Larkin Mead of the Stanford family (now located next to the Mausoleum). In 1902 or early 1903 she placed four large Japanese bronzes as "illustrative of higher Japanese life" in the corner of the court. Two were bronze vases, each weighing several tons and representing the "Buddhist idea of Heaven, the Earth, and Hell." Two others were moved here from other sites on campus, and included a ring of elephants supporting a pagoda and an eagle perched on a vine-clad stump "intimidating monkeys about the base." Jane Stanford had purchased the bronzes during a trip to Japan, but they have since been displaced.

　　Screened behind surrounding arcades, the court mediates between the long axis of Palm Drive and the grand space of the Inner Quad courtyard. Jane Stanford dedicated the court in 1900 with a plaque on the west wall honoring those Stanford volunteers of the Spanish-American War of 1898. The memorial service for Leland Stanford, who died on June 21, 1893, was held under the gabled arch at the south end of the court, and Jane Stanford's own funeral procession marched through the court in 1905 en route to the mausoleum in the arboretum. Rodin's Burghers of Calais, 1884–95, now grace the southeast lawn.

Palm Drive Entry

Approaching Stanford: Planning Around the Oval

Immediately north of the Outer Quad along the fringes of the arboretum, Jane Stanford erected several monumental structures of which only two survive, the museum and chemistry buildings (a library and gymnasium were destroyed in the 1906 earthquake). Together, they formed a wonderfully bizarre collection of Victorian architectural confectionery, a Shangri-la of glistening domes and hybrid styles easily at home in a world's fair. This curious compendium, mostly built after Leland Stanford's death, began the change from his development of a unified architectural setting.

Coolidge wanted the Outer Quad to "explode," as he said, upon the viewer from the north end of the Oval, where Olmsted's teardrop-shaped sunken lawn deflected the processional approach of Palm Drive. A vista of buildings and landscape suddenly spreads out along the horizon. Olmsted planted only low shrubs in the Oval to enhance the effect. Graduated terracing reveals the extent to which the north front stands above grade, visually relieving the squatness of the long horizontal row of buildings, according to Olmsted.

The early university sat in the midst of paddocks, agricultural lands, and open fields. Leland Stanford envisioned these fields, along with the horse farm, as outdoor laboratories for various departments within the university. The lands were to support a large agriculture program, though Stanford later reduced its importance as his educational mission became clearer. Olmsted's plan to forest the foothills south of the university was overruled by Stanford, who felt it would have destroyed a virgin California landscape. Olmsted's proposal to establish a "university forest" to the north, between the university gates and the Outer Quad, was more successful though this was later absorbed into a more ambitious "arboretum," an area organized by specimens of exotic of trees and plants. Leland Stanford had wanted specimens of every type of tree that could be grown in the Mediterranean-like climate of Palo Alto and proposed encircling the campus with a representative universal forest. Thomas Douglas planted Olmsted's extensive wilderness between 1889 and 1892. Without Olmsted's presence, or that of Leland Stanford after 1893, the original landscaping was neglected, and the eucalyptus trees, selected as "nurse trees"—the most prominent planting in the arboretum—generally overwhelmed the more delicate, exotic plants they were meant to shelter (before they could be selectively removed). Ironically, several Australian-native pests have recently decimated the eucalyptus species in the Arboretum, leading to a replanting of native California species, such as oak and buckeye.

Efforts to restore the Arboretum were made in the 1910s and 1920s, with mixed results and at a time when the number of species, originally planned to be in the thousands, had dwindled to fewer than two hundred. In 1914, Olmsted's firm, since assumed by his sons, was commissioned to restore the grounds and its buildings, especially the arboretum. In the 1920s, Gardner Dailey, who had apprenticed with John McLaren, superintendent of Golden Gate Park in San Francisco, was hired as the university's landscape architect. He drew up a master plan to restore the arboretum for scientific study of botany and forestry and renewed the wildflowers in this region. Dailey also created the current Oval with its central pedestrian paths and a central pool, since replaced with seasonal planting. His removal of red geraniums bordering the oval caused an uproar over the loss of plantings that were seen as historic and symbolic, but were particularly vulnerable to drought.

Presidents Branner (1913–15) and Wilbur (1916–43) both undertook to improve the grounds in general by removing "temporary" buildings scattered over the campus and by planting shrubs, flowers, and vines around the university's main buildings. These efforts included grading and planting the areas between the Inner and Outer Quads. At this time, many of the campus's open spaces were covered with low-growing shrubs designed to give the impression of green lawns. This included cotoneaster and other shrubs planted along the front of the Outer Quad by Ivan Nyquist, the university's gardener and grounds foreman.

10. Iris & B. Gerald Cantor Center for Visual Arts at Stanford University (formerly Stanford University Museum of Art)

George Washington Percy and Frederick F. Hamilton, 1890; north and south annexes, 1898–1899; Charles Hodges and Clinton Day, north, south, and west annexes, 1902–1906; Polshek and Partners, restoration and addition, 1996–1998

Iris and B. Gerald Cantor Center for Visual Arts

The old Stanford Museum was the other of two monuments dedicated by the Stanfords to the memory of their son, a precocious collector. The building is inspired by the National Archaeological Museum (1860) in Athens, which Leland Junior had visited shortly before his death, and consists of a domed central block with an Ionic portico and stepped-back wings and projecting pedimented end blocks. The building was the earliest classical museum in America, as well as a pioneering work of reinforced concrete by Ernest Ransome. Its patented construction introduced the technique of embedding twisted iron rods with raised surfaces, which prevented slipping in the concrete, and is the precursor of today's reinforced concrete construction technique. The Stanfords adopted this method of construction because of the urgent need to complete the building for the opening of the university in October 1891 and the higher cost of a conventional masonry building.

Jane Stanford oversaw the museum's design and construction, which included additional wings and rotundas enclosing a quadrangle. By 1905 the museum had grown to 200,000 square feet, making it perhaps the largest in the United States. The additions, however, were largely built of unreinforced brick rather than reinforced concrete and only portions survived the 1906 quake. (The north and south rotundas were rebuilt following the 1989 earthquake, though the western wing with its circular rotunda, which no longer serves the museum, remains closed. The Rodin Sculpture Garden sits on the foundations of the collapsed south annex and rotunda.)

Ransome credited Leland Stanford with aiding in the development of concrete technology. Stanford was concerned that during an earthquake, the sixty-foot-tall Ionic columns of the central portico would collapse and instructed the workmen to construct them from a continuous pour (a remarkable innovation at this time) so that seamless, monolithic shafts were created. The lobby boasted the longest reinforced concrete beams at the time, supporting a 46-by-56-foot skylight and roof. During the most recent restoration, it was discovered that Ransome's system was more experimental than previously believed: the reinforcing rods were irregularly rather than uniformly twisted, having been turned by hand on the site; the exterior walls were actually unreinforced load-bearing concrete; and much of the reinforcement had been overlapped, an unexpected innovation at this early date. Ransome was less daring in adopting the convention of treating concrete surfaces as "artificial stone," though he left the aggregate exposed as an aesthetic property. Ransome felt the concrete roof was a significant achievement, though it leaked continually until it was eventually covered over by sheetmetal.

Originally, sculptures of Plutarch, Aristotle, Herodotus, and Plato by M. A. Edwards lined the roof parapet, though these were destroyed in the 1906 quake. The figures of Menander and Faith flanking the central entry are by Antonio Frilli, an Italian artist. Also on the exterior of the wings and over the main entry are mosaic panels Jane Stanford commissioned between 1902 and 1904 from Salviati and Company in Venice. They reflect the Stanfords' interest in the mechanical arts (Painting, Sculpture, Architecture) and antiquity (Archaeology, Egypt, Cypress, Rome). The pedagogic mission of the university is echoed in the depiction of Progress and Civilization, recalling the sculpted frieze of Memorial Arch, representing the Progress of Civilization in America.

The Renaissance palazzo-like lobby is a startling contrast; it is a coolly ornate skylit space dominated by a grand staircase, terrazzo floor, and interior walls paneled in gray marble veneer and lined by white pilaster strips. The statue of Athena at the head of the lobby staircase is also by Frilli and was commissioned by Jane Stanford. A second-story arcaded balcony, once displaying copies of classical busts, is ringed by a cornice from which spring flared arches below a flat, coffered ceiling and a shallow dome. The long, narrow ground floor galleries feature columned Egyptian and Doric exedrae, and the unpartitioned upper floor galleries are skylit under arched ceilings with curving, exposed-truss steel beams. The museum once boasted advanced engineering systems, including built-in small electric lights in the galleries.

Polshek & Partners' recent metal-and-glass addition consciously contrasts with the older building's seemingly impenetrable exterior, opening onto outdoor sculpture gardens and an inner garden court. The textured stucco surfaces and sandstone-like coloring as well as proportional corre-spondences marry the two buildings compatibly. A circular terrace, facing the northern contemporary sculpture garden, is partially surrounded by a curved wall, a reference to the museum's history and fragmentary state.

11. Chemistry Building (closed) *Clinton Day, 1900–1902*

Chemistry Building

The Chemistry Building is the only significant structure on campus designed entirely by Clinton Day, a San Francisco architect who designed many projects for Jane Stanford. He designed Geology Corner; and he modified Coolidge's design for Memorial Church, earning Jane Stanford's enmity over its protracted construction and cost. Day's design is likely adapted from plans for a chemistry building by Hodges reviewed by Leland Stanford shortly before his death in 1893. The Chemistry Building—with its rough-faced ashlar sandstone construction; pseudo-Mission details (the squat, towerlike forms that flank the central entry and red-tile roof); and Romanesque elements (the arcuated upper windows, decorative rosettes, and flat pilaster strips)—relates more immediately to the Main Quad than the other more eclectic buildings that were in this region before the 1906 earthquake, although it clearly appears to mitigate contextually between the Main Quad's Mission–Romanesque styling to the south and the Museum's neoclassicism to the north. The building suffered moderate damage in 1906 and was quickly repaired. It was closed in 1986 because of fire safety hazards and awaits renovation for some future use. In the rear was the Assay laboratory, reached through an enclosed courtyard; this was demolished when the Stauffer labs were constructed in 1960.

12. Library
Joseph Evan Mackay, with Clinton Day (revisions), 1902–1906; destroyed, 1906

Library and Gymnasium (1905)

Opposite the Museum and Chemistry buildings, the library and the gymnasium were among the largest and most expensive buildings erected by Jane Stanford to fall in the 1906 quake. Located on the site now occupied by the Graduate School of Business, the new library was to supersede the Thomas Welton Stanford Library in the northeast range of the Outer Quad, only two years after the earlier library's completion. After a competition for the building, Jane Stanford surprised her architects by choosing an entry by a San Francisco art glassmaker, Joseph MacKay. His curious blend of classical and Romanesque elements captured Jane Stanford's imagination, and Clinton Day was hired to oversee the building's construction but was forbidden to alter the design (of which only a perspective sketch was submitted). The interior contained a large central rotunda capped by a tall dome set on a steel frame, inspired by the newly completed Library of Congress in Washington, D. C. As the building neared completion, its poor structural design and construction methods were detected. Shortly after Jane Stanford's death in 1905, the university tried to remedy some of the problems by removing the luxurious woodwork inside to further fireproof the building and by adding steel to strengthen the unreinforced masonry walls, modifications that might have lessened the damage from the quake had they been completed in time.

13. Gymnasium   *Charles Hodges, 1902–1906; destroyed, 1906*

Planned at the same time as the new library, the half-million-dollar gymnasium would have been the largest in the United States. Sited north of the library and directly across Palm Drive from the museum, it echoed the museum's formal, neoclassical style. Hodges employed cast-iron columns throughout and an iron truss roof over the main gymnasium. Like the library, a prominent, glazed dome, reflecting Jane Stanford's taste for monumental, if structurally insubstantial, architecture (the building was also built largely of unreinforced brick) surmounted the gym. Copies of Canova's Pugilist and Wrestler (executed by Bartholdi) flanked the entrance portico. The interior was richly detailed in white marble and tile. The building contained a swimming tank, handball courts, bowling alleys, and a large gymnasium. However, Jane Stanford envisioned the building as a social center, reserving its top floor for a ballroom (the dance floor was cushioned by springs) with kitchen facilities and a banquet hall. There

Gymnasium, Lasuen Street (1906)

was also a meeting room for the trustees, a trophy room, and the library of the hygiene department. Remnants of the original foundations can still be seen at its site, which remains as open space adjacent to Frost Amphitheater.

14. Mausoleum   *Caterson and Clark, 1887–1888*

This elegant little Roman Ionic temple of polished Vermont granite is a more modest version of an earlier design that, according to newspaper accounts, would have rivaled the grand structures of Jay Gould and the Vanderbilts. The site of the mausoleum may have determined the orientation of the university. Early in the planning of the university, Olmsted ran the main axis of the Inner Quad roughly north-south ending in an existing cemetery to the south, where he planned a significant road through the site with the mausoleum at its head. As the plan evolved, the mausoleum was moved behind Memorial Church and then onto an axis at the head of what was to become Palm Drive directly opposite the church. Its current site removed the mausoleum from any direct planning relationship to the university's system of axes when the Stanfords determined that Palm Drive should proceed unimpeded to the Palo Alto train station.

The four-acre site, landscaped by Olmsted, was originally chosen for the Stanfords' new house, but the plan was abandoned and the mausoleum erected after the death of Leland Junior. (According to David Starr Jordan's wife, the Stanfords had contracted with H. H. Richardson to design their "country mansion" before their plans changed.) The building is set on a low

Mausoleum

mound and raised on a high base approached by a flight of steps guarded by sphinxes (alluding to Leland Junior's perspicacity), which also appear at the back (originally these sphinxes once flanked the entrance, but were moved when Jane Stanford had new figures carved).

Four freestanding Ionic columns, coupled on either side of the tomb door, and corner pilasters support a plain architrave and closed pediment. The freestanding columns, which continue round the sides and back, are set close to the wall, adding a sense of grandeur to this serene tomb. Originally, several avenues radiated from the tomb (only the main vista towards what was once Peter Coutts's farm, Pine Lane, is still visible), marking it as an important focal point in the plan. To the northeast was a small cemetery for faculty and students, which was removed in the 1910s. And to the south is the remnant of the formally laid out Arizona or Cactus Garden, planted in the early 1880s and restored in 1998.

15. Firehouse (Fire-Truck House)

Charles Hodges, 1904; Logan Hopper Associates, renovation, 1996

Firehouse

This two-story Greek Revival style building served as the campus firehouse until the early 1960s, when a separate fire facility was built on Serra Street. Originally, the first floor housed the hook-and-ladder truck and the second floor was home to volunteers and one professional firefighter. About 1940 the building was expanded and a five-story drill tower was also added. In 1996 the firehouse was modified to conform to disabled access requirements, including the addition of an elevator. Today the building houses several student campus organizations.

16. Bookstore *Arthur B. Clark, 1905; renovations, Page & Turnbull, 2006*

Stanford's earliest bookstore consisted of a wood shack erected by students near Green Library in 1891. Created as a cooperative association, the bookstore shared its profits with its customers. In 1897 the faculty recognized the need for a more substantial structure and had a new building constructed on the corner of Panama Street and Lomita Drive, near the current site of the Stanford University Press. In 1905 Arthur Clark, who taught drawing and drafting in the graphic art department at Stanford, designed a larger bookstore in the Spanish mission style with brick and plaster walls and red tile roof on an "imposing site" at the end of Alvarado Row, behind the Main Quad. Clark's design consisted of two separate buildings housing the bookstore along Lasuen and behind it, across a narrow alley, was the office and stores selling candy, ice cream, and groceries. The two buildings were joined in 1929. This "main street" structure was originally a juncture between the faculty and student housing areas and the main academic area. Occupied by the Career Development Center for many years, the building will undergo renovation and reopen in 2006 as the Barnum Family Center for School and Community Partnerships.

17. Boiler House and Engineering Buildings

Shepley, Rutan, and Coolidge, with Charles Hodges, 1887–1891

These utilitarian structures immediately behind the quad provided the first university buildings with electric light and steam heat powered by the boiler house, whose tall chimneystack collapsed in the 1906 quake. In style, the buildings mimic the Spanish-Romanesque of the quad, with their rough-faced sandstone or brick masonry and red tile roofs with central light monitors. These airy sheds now serve as research and teaching space and most have recently been restored and refurbished.

Boiler House

18. Encina and Roble Gymnasiums, 1891–1892

Olmsted's original plan provided for athletic fields within an east quad for men and playing fields to the west for women. The site of the university's current main library had initially served Stanford's athletic activities. Two temporary shingle buildings on either side of the campus near the men's and women's respective dorms were quickly designed and erected to accommodate the university's athletic programs. Following protests in the 1920s by women athletes, who complained about its dilapidated condition and cramped single room without heating, Roble was replaced in the 1930s by a new building designed by Bakewell and Brown. The spaces of the old "Woodpecker Lodge," as it was popularly known for the birds who pecked away at the shingled exterior, were used for a variety of purposes through the years, including housing portions of the fine art department, before being razed in 1957. Encina was never completely finished, and in 1894, male students paid for the addition of a single shower-bath. Handball courts were added in 1899. It was to be replaced by the new gymnasium, which fell in the 1906 quake.

Nature Intervenes

Main Quad, post earthquake (1906)

Chemistry Building and Museum, post earthquake (1906)

In 1906, a little more than a year after the death of Jane Stanford, and as the university moved to complete the last buildings planned and initiated by the founders, the great San Francisco earthquake struck. This natural calamity destroyed or damaged many of the most outstanding campus structures—Memorial Arch, Memorial Church, the Outer Quad, the nearly completed library and gymnasium, the vast additions to the museum, and the chemistry building. Damage to the Inner Quad was less severe (Charles Coolidge attributed this to Leland Stanford's mandate to use broad foundations under his buildings, and he criticized Jane Stanford for abandoning this safeguard). An engineers' report commissioned by the university after the quake revealed that the worst damage occurred to those buildings constructed of unreinforced brick, notably those commissioned by Jane Stanford.

Library and Gymnasium, post earthquake (1906)

From the beginning, the Stanfords envisioned a residential university housing its students and faculty. Initially Leland Stanford planned to adopt Olmsted's "cottage system," large houses each accommodating about twenty-five students and a faculty member. However, building the university had taken longer and required greater resources than anticipated, obviating Olmsted's plan and delaying the construction of both dorms and faculty housing to a late date.

Alvarado Row (1892)

In 1889, only two years from the university's scheduled opening, Stanford commissioned two large dorms to provide housing for almost five hundred students. The dorms, Encina for men, to the east of the Main Quad, and Roble for women, equidistant to the west, were built along Serra Mall, consciously enforcing a common, if casual, segregation of the sexes. (At one point during planning, Francis Walker, president of M. I. T., who had consulted with Stanford on the planning of the university, recommended as a practical matter locating men's departments, such as engineering, and women's departments, essentially the humanities, nearest their respective dorms, though this was never strictly implemented.)

By the mid-1890s students had organized themselves into fraternities (twenty had been created both on and off campus by 1895, housing 190 students), and a string of houses was built along Alvarado Row and Mayfield, providing additional residences for students and faculty on campus and eventually accommodating two-thirds of the campus's student population (Jordan liked the sense of community and student-faculty interaction that the proximity of mixed housing provided). The houses were mission, neoclassical, or shingle in style. Many students still found housing with faculty off campus either in Mayfield or Palo Alto, and the construction camp, which provided housing for some students from the opening of the university, was renamed Palmetto Hall about 1892 and used as a student residence and eating club until its competition with the university's Stanford Inn (Charles Hodges, 1898) in 1902 proved serious enough to warrant its razing.

While Leland Stanford had delayed construction of faculty housing until after the major buildings neared completion, he then rushed to build ten identical houses, adapted from pattern books by Charles E. Hodges, along Alvarado Row before the opening of the university. Olmsted's original plans called for housing tracts platted along curving roads to the southeast, Alvarado Row, Salvatierra and Lasuen Streets, and Mayfield Avenue.

Alvarado area neighborhood view

Olmsted wrote Stanford that each street might have a different style of architecture, though this suggestion was never carried out.

Building a house on campus had its problems: the land could not be purchased, only leased, encouraging some faculty to reside in Palo Alto. (Professorville, as it is called today, is the earliest subdivision in Palo Alto, dating from the 1890s, and is where some faculty chose to live. For their designs they turned primarily to Arthur B. Clark, who had designed the bookstore and later, the Hoover House, and Charles Edward Hodges, an architect who had worked for Shepley, Rutan, and Coolidge during the design of the university and was later hired by the Stanfords as their unofficial campus architect.) More difficult for the faculty was the stipulation that a campus house could not fall below a certain cost, making houses relatively expensive. Nevertheless, some forty houses had been built by 1893. Clark and Hodges designed many of the earliest residences (those built between 1891 and 1906), including fraternities.

The compactness and concentration of Stanford's earliest faculty and student housing, as well as later nearby subdivisions, such as San Juan Hill, Lagunita Knoll, and Pine Hill I and II (see Part 6), make walking tours feasible. For this reason, a list of addresses with their architects is given for a particular street in addition to a description of the more significant or interesting houses.

For the reader's convenience, houses in the Mayfield Avenue area built after 1906 are included in this section. Please respect residents' privacy; most houses are private and not open to the public.

19. Encina Hall and Encina Commons

Encina Hall, Shepley, Rutan, and Coolidge, 1889–1891; Encina Commons, Bakewell and Brown, 1923; Major renovations, Hardy, Holzman, Pfeiffer, 1996–1998

Encina Hall

The early student dorms at Stanford consisted of two hotel-like buildings that were fitted out with the most modern conveniences, including electricity, steam heat, a dining hall, and a lounge. In fact, Encina was modeled after a Swiss hotel the Stanfords had visited in 1888 that partly inspired Coolidge's design, although Encina's Richardsonian Romanesque style, which features an arcade along the main entry, appropriately harmonized the building with the Inner Quad. Initially Coolidge planned tall campanile-like towers and a more pronounced E-shaped plan enclosing the front court, though these were eliminated at Stanford's request. Encina was regarded as a luxury dorm when opened, with 315 students paying $23 a month for room and board. Immediately beyond the columned entry vestibule was a short flight of steps leading into the double-height dining hall with its amber-colored skylight, large fireplace, and smaller flanking serving rooms. The dining hall was served from the basement kitchen, where were also located the

Encina Hall, Dining Room

servants' hall, the men's room, and the "Chinaman's room." However, the long, double-loaded corridors, with their large numbers of students on each floor, invited hazing, roughhousing, and even riots. By 1893 newspapers were already reporting "fiendish noises" emanating from the hall. And in the following year, in an effort to improve dining and student life in the dorms, both Encina and Roble were operated as cooperatives run by the students and faculty. In 1898 the university opened the Stanford Inn, a restaurant providing lodging and board, replacing Encina's dining facilities, which had ceased operation the previous year. Encina's hall was converted into a clubroom with billiard tables, becoming the first student center. Recently, this space, after being abandoned for many years, was restored with its original wood paneling and fireplace to house the Bechtel Conference Center.

Following repeated riots, Encina was remodeled in 1916 and ninety rooms added. New dorms were constructed in the 1910s and 1920s with smaller hall units, moving closer to Olmsted's intention. In the 1920s, as the university built new men's dorms, Encina was given over exclusively to housing freshmen, who were required to reside there for the year. Encina's usefulness as a residence ended in the 1950s when Branner Hall was opened and the old dorm was remodeled as an administrative building. In 1972 a fire, started either carelessly or maliciously, severely damaged the east wing, and only recently (1996–98) has the building been restored and reoccupied as the home of the Stanford Institute for International Studies.

20. Roble Hall, later Sequoia Hall

Percy and Hamilton, with Ernest Ransome, 1891; demolished, 1996

Roble Hall (1892)

Stanford University was planned as a coeducational institution. Jane Stanford claimed after her husband's death that she had persuaded him to admit women as well as men, necessitating the hasty construction of Roble Hall, the women's dorm. However, this story is disputed by her private secretary, Bertha Berner, who wrote that Leland Stanford argued for the admission of women on educational grounds from an early date, an assertion supported by newspaper articles, which from the outset, noted that the university was to be coeducational.

Whatever the truth, a large women's dorm of sandstone construction, the same size as Encina was begun, but the dorm was abandoned when it was realized that it would not be ready by opening day ceremonies. More resources were devoted to completing Encina and building a smaller, three-story women's dorm on a site closer to the Main Quad rather than postpone the admission of women (the Stanfords felt that later acceptance would seem an afterthought). The firm of Percy and Hamilton, then building the museum using Ernest Ransome's reinforced-concrete system, adopted it for Roble, completing it in ninety-seven days and in time for the university's opening in October 1891. Roble housed eighty students, the anticipated enrollment of women, although this entailed the conversion at the last minute of the attic story into additional rooms lighted by dormer windows. The parlor, distinctive of women's dorms, was described as being a large, long room pale blue and pink in color with fireplaces at either end flanked by a "pink and blue chairs with large ribbon bows."

Women were required to live on campus, and as enrollment increased additional cottage-style houses were renovated into women's residences. In 1899 Jane Stanford placed a cap of five hundred on the number of women students admitted, and this limit stood until 1933. A larger women's dorm was not built until 1918, when a new Roble replaced the older one, which was then renamed Sequoia Hall and served as a men's dorm until World War II. By the 1940s the building had become decrepit, and in 1951 Spencer and Ambrose was hired to remove its upper floors, leaving only the ground story, and to convert it for the Applied Mathematics and Statistics Laboratory. The remaining portion of the building was demolished in 1996 to make way for the Science and Engineering Quad development. A new Sequoia Hall was built nearby to replace its functions as the home of the Statistics Department.

21. Alvarado Row, Salvatierra Walk, Lasuen Street, and Mayfield Avenue Houses

Most of the student residences and administrative or academic buildings along Alvarado Row, Salvatierra Walk, Lasuen Street, and Mayfield Avenue, as well as houses on other streets further south, were constructed as faculty residences. These were large houses, designed primarily in the turn-of-the-century shingle style, as faculty members were encouraged to provide student accommodations in their homes.

As the houses began to be converted to other uses, they were often enlarged in stages. In some cases the exteriors were enlarged several times. When one of these houses (Lathrop House at 543 Lasuen Street) underwent a renovation in 1993, demolition of certain areas indicated that the house had been enlarged in outward layers, somewhat onionlike. Most Row houses do not, therefore, reflect their original size or exterior form. However a few examples do remain in which the original structure is clearly discernible.

Griffen–Drell House, 570 Alvarado Row

Griffen-Drell House, 570 Alvarado Row *(Charles Hodges, 1892)*
A pattern-book house that was duplicated with the Owen House at 553
Salvatierra Walk, it is a rigidly symmetrical shingle style house with twin
conical-roofed turrets. Until 2005 this was the oldest house on campus to
remain a private residence.

Chi Theta Chi, 576 Alvarado Row *(original architect unknown, circa 1896)*
Mediterranean-style stucco building with Spanish Colonial details, this is
presently a student cooperative house.

579 Alvarado Row *(Theodore W. Lenzen, 1930)* This shingle style house
with half-timbering and stucco gables, serves as a private residence today.
It was refurbished in 1988 by Morgan, Mitchael Construction.

Bolivar House, 582 Alvarado Row *(Curtis Tobey, 1898)* Shingle and half-
timbered house with a decorative frieze over the first-story windows and
squat, Doric columns on one corner, which serves as the Center for Latin
American Studies.

Hammarskjold House, 592 Alvarado Row *(architect unknown, 1896;
Brocchini Architects, renovation, 1994)* A large, stylish neoclassical house with a
curving two-story portico of Corinthian columns. It is a lapboard house
with quoins, which serves as a student cooperative residence today.
Believed to have been constructed as a faculty residence, this house has
gone through several enlargements and renovations, including the addition of a third story and wings.

Mariposa House, 546 Salvatierra Walk *(Charles Hodges, 1892)* Mariposa House is a shingle style house at one time occupied by graduate women. In 1964 it was repaired and opened for academic office use, and now serves as the Law Center.

Rogers House, 549 Salvatierra Walk *(architect unknown, 1892)* Originally built as a shingle-sided faculty residence of two stories and attic, this house was occupied as a private residence until 1976, when it became office for several university functions. The house was once the home of Herbert Nash, who served as Leland Stanford Junior's private tutor before becoming the senior Stanford's private secretary and later the university librarian. In 1976 the house was renovated for the Center for Research in International Studies; it now houses the Bridge, a peer counseling center.

Owen House, 553 Salvatierra Walk *(Charles Hodges, circa 1896)* This twin to the Griffin-Drell House was built originally as a boarding house. It was sold as a private residence in 1927, changed to academic uses in 1957, and now serves as a Law School annex.

Serra House, 556 Salvatierra Walk *(Birge Clark, 1923)* Built for Stanford's first president, David Starr Jordan, in a Spanish adobe-style, the house was moved to its present site from its former location at the western end of Serra Street in 1983 when the Central Energy Facility was built. It now houses the Institute for Research on Women and Gender.

Gould Center for Conflict Resolution, after major renovation, 1996–1997

Martin Daniel Gould Center for Conflict Resolution Programs (Huston House), 575 Salvatierra Walk *(William P. Knowles, circa 1889; Page and Turnbull, renovation, 1996–1997)* Professor Charles A. Huston of the Law School was an early resident of the house. In 1972 it was converted to academic and administrative uses. Damaged in the 1989 earthquake, it has subsequently been restored and is currently occupied by the Law School for academic programs.

Lathrop House, 543 Lasuen Street *(architect unknown, 1896; Lee and Lee, major renovation, 1993)* Built as a faculty residence in the Queen Anne style, the house had a corner turret and a gambrel roof with front and side porches. Alterations and modification over the years leaves little of the original structure discernible. It was last renovated in 1993 by Lee and Lee, architects, and now serves as the student residence, Muwekma-Tah-Ruk, which has a program emphasis in Native American studies.

Storey House, 544 Lasuen Street *(Wolfe and McKenzie, 1896; Sigurd Lorenzen Rupp, major renovation, 1981)* A Colonial Revival house with Doric pilasters and fanlight used as a student residence, the house was severely damaged by fire in 1980 and reconstructed.

Stillman House, 549 Lasuen Street *(Thorp and Lenzen, 1896; John K. Branner, renovation, 1930; Lee and Lee, renovation, 1993)* Originally a shingle style house, it acquired its current appearance in the 1930s when John K. Branner remodeled it for the Kappa Alpha Theta sorority, for which it received an Honor Award from the Northern Chapter of the American Institute of Architects. A Greek Revival house, it features an inset, two-story portico of square Doric posts and paired-end chimneys. The house was moved in 1975 from its original location; it remains a student cooperative residence, named Columbae.

Sigma Chi, 550 Lasuen Street *(John K. Branner, 1938)* A Colonial Revival house with large swan's neck doorframe over Doric pilasters and a fanlight, it still serves as a fraternity house.

553 Mayfield Avenue *(Arthur Clark, 1894; Swatt Architects, renovation, 1994)* A Colonial Revival house with a curved pediment over the door and quoins decorating the corners, it was moved from its original location on Lasuen Street to its present site in 1975.

557 Mayfield Avenue *(architect unknown, 1896; Lee and Lee, renovation, 1993)*

557 Mayfield Avenue (1998)

A Greek Revival house with a two-story curving portico of square Doric posts, it continues as a student residence.

Dunn–Bacon House (1998)

Dunn-Bacon House, 565 Mayfield Avenue *(Charles Hodges, 1899; renovations, Hoover Associates, 2004)* This is a large, white, board-and-batten, neoclassical house with a two-story, pedimented portico and coupled Ionic columns. Grander than most faculty houses of the day, it was actually built for a friend of Jane Stanford's who had no official affiliation with the university. (Harriet Dunn operated a boarding house for young faculty in a separate building on the campus). The shuttered windows are distinctive of Dunn's Boston home, which she asked Hodges to recall in his design. The house is well preserved, retaining most of its original interiors and their fixtures. A family member, Professor Harold M. Bacon acquired the property in 1930, and the university recently purchased it from the Bacon family. The house was renovated and reopened in 2005 as the Taube Hillel House at the Harold and Libby Ziff Center for Jewish Life.

Grove–Lasuen House (1998)

Grove-Lasuen House, 572 Mayfield Avenue *(Charles E. Hodges, 1896; Lee and Lee, renovation, 1994)* A uniquely designed neoclassical duplex residence of lapped-board siding with porticos of coupled Ionic columns and pilasters supporting second-story, balustraded balconies. Along Mayfield Avenue, a projecting section is framed by a giant order of Ionic pilaster strips set under a deep, bracketed pediment, though the offset entrance portico is idiosyncratic. The dormer along the Campus Drive facade contains a sunburst motif in its gable. The building was used as a fraternity house in 1971; in 1994 the duplex was remodeled into a single student residence.

Phi Sig, 1018 Campus Drive *(architect unknown, 1896; Burks, Toma Architects, renovation, 1994)* Originally the barn of the Cooksey Estate at 550 San Juan Street, this sprawling house with its gambrel roof has been remodeled many times to accommodate student residents. While retaining its Phi Sig name, it has served as a general student residence for many years.

Grove-Mayfield House, 584 Mayfield Avenue *(Wright, Rushforth, and Cahill, 1907; Lee and Lee, renovation, 1995)* A Spanish eclectic style house with portico, tiled roof, and shuttered windows, it serves as a student residence.

Kairos House, 586 Mayfield Avenue *(A. W. Smith, 1911; Architectural Resources Group, renovation, 1996)* Originally constructed for the Delta Chi fraternity, this student residence was acquired by the university in the 1970s.

592 Mayfield Avenue *(A. W. Smith, 1912; Cody Anderson Wasney, renovation, 1996)* Originally built for the Alpha Tau Omega fraternity, this student residence was acquired by the university in 1968 and since that time has housed the Delta Kappa Epsilon fraternity and served as a general student residence. It is now occupied by the Phi Kappa Psi fraternity.

La Maison Française, 610 Mayfield Avenue *(architect unknown, 1909; Architectural Resources Group, renovation, 1996)* Modified Dutch revival style with bow porch arches (later infilled with windows), this shingle-sided house has been modified with an additional wing, although most of the original structure and proportions remain intact. Original occupants were members of the Pi Beta Phi sorority. Following the abolition of sororities, the house was renamed The Chalet (1944) and then Guthrie House (1945). Since 1975, this residence has been La Maison Française, occupied by students who are studying or who have an interest in the French language and culture.

Jordan House-Haus Mitteleuropa, 620 Mayfield Avenue *(A. W. Smith, 1910; Swatt Architects, renovation, 1995)* Originally a two-story shingled craftsman style sorority house with a large gable and porches at the upper levels, this house went through several expansions during the 1930s, which modified the exterior and left none of the original remaining. It is now a student residence for those with a program emphasis in European studies.

Gardinier Apartments, 624 Mayfield Avenue *(architect unknown, 1921)*A contemporary variant of the Spanish eclectic style distinguished by a metal grille balcony with twisted columns and segmental arched windows, this is an apartment building used by faculty and staff.

Durand House, 634 Mayfield Avenue *(Charles K. Sumner, 1911)* A modified Tudor style house, with additions of wings and other minor modifications, which have not significantly altered the original exterior massing and fenestration of this student residence.

Hurlburt House-Slavianskii Dom, 650 Mayfield Avenue *(architect unknown, 1900; Swatt Architects, renovation, 1995)* A shingled, Colonial Revival house with a full-length porch supported by thin Roman Doric columns, the house was moved from the site of the Pearce Mitchell housing complex to this location in 1974. It serves as a student residence today with a program emphasis in East European Studies.

Roth House, 713 Santa Ynez *(architect unknown, 1910)* Originally a modified craftsman style, two-story, shingle-sided house for the Gamma Phi Beta sorority, major additions and exterior modifications have been made to the residence, resulting in a modified Tudor style, board-and-batten house with half-timbering and stucco. Roth House now serves as a women's student residence.

Theta Xi, 717 Dolores *(architect unknown, 1915)* Theta Xi was the original occupant of this federal style house with pedimented Doric portico, decorative frieze, and dormers with alternatively pointed and curved pediments. It currently serves as an undergraduate student residence, named Taxi.

Durand-Kirkman House, 623 Cabrillo Street *(Arthur B. Clark, 1904)* A large shingle style house designed around an old oak tree, this residence is typical of the style in its picturesque massing and details, gambrel roofs, bay windows, covered porches, and seemingly arbitrarily positioned window and door openings. Constructed of redwood, the house features hand-carved details of flowers by the architect. The house was originally owned by William F. Durand, a pioneer in the field of aeronautics at Stanford. It is a private residence.

22. Cooksey House (Synergy), 550 San Juan Street

Charles Hodges, 1901; Hardy, Holzman, Pfeiffer, major restoration, 1993

A large shingle style house with gambrel roofs, the Cooksey House stands near the crest of San Juan Hill and was built for a friend of Jane Stanford who was unaffiliated with the university. After Mrs. Cooksey's death the house was presented to Stanford as a potential hospital, though the university never used it as such. The house was beautifully restored after suffering severe damage in the 1989 earthquake and now serves as a student cooperative called Synergy.

23. Lathrop Gatehouse 1900

Charles Lathrop was Jane Stanford's brother and assisted her with her building campaign after 1898. All that remains of the seventeen-acre Charles Lathrop estate on the knoll, located southwest of the Stock Farm, are a few barns and this large gatehouse, visible from the intersection of Junipero Serra Boulevard and Campus Drive West. The main house was razed in the 1950s to make for the Center for Advanced Study in the Behavioral Sciences.

Lathrop Gatehouse

OPPOSITE: *Cooksey House*

The Beaux Arts Era: 1906–1940

Hoover Tower and Green Library

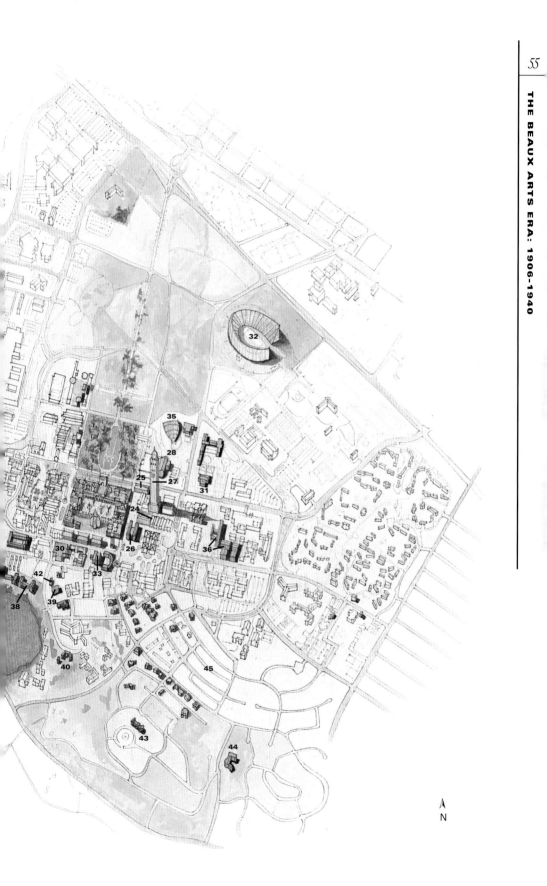

N

Campus Planning, 1906–1940

The founders' halcyon years of building ended ruinously with the 1906 San Francisco earthquake. During the period of reconstruction, which lasted through the 1910s, the university restored its essential structures—the dorms, the inner and outer quads, and the chemistry building—followed by its more symbolic buildings—Memorial Church and the museum. The quake had a significant impact on Stanford's campus planning; it checked the piecemeal building initiated by Jane Stanford and spurred the university to return to the planning order of the Quad, albeit without the seemingly endless resources of its founders. Indeed, the outstanding personal features of the specific memorializing and pedagogic programs of the Stanfords, embedded in their planning ideals of the Quad, were for the university no longer memorable, appealing, or possible. (This was clear in the decision not to rebuild Memorial Arch or the original tower of Memorial Church, although rebuilding was contemplated initially.)

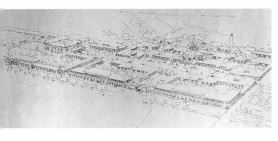

Bird's Eye Perspective of Bakewell and Brown's New Quadrangle (1916)

Significant thoughts about new building, signaling a period of renewed vigor, did not occur until 1913, when proposals for a library quad were first studied. The university tried to order its architectural expansion by adopting the quad as an organizing principle and by hiring the San Francisco firm of Bakewell and Brown (which in 1912 had won the competition to design the San Francisco City Hall) as consulting architects, a position it held for almost thirty years. Bakewell and Brown's work initiated the tradition of adopting the most distinctive elements of the quad buildings— the arcades, the buff-colored and articulated walls, and the red-tile roofs—as a unifying and ubiquitous architectural theme.

John Bakewell believed that the red-tile roofs especially offered a "powerful and invaluable" unifying element between older buildings and newer ones, which for functional and economic reasons had to employ contemporary materials and structural systems, such as reinforced concrete and steel frames concealed behind sandstone or rough plaster-veneered walls. Tile roofs, according to Bakewell, were timeless and had been used with "practically every style and period so there was no difficulty in incorporating it in any modified version [i.e., modern architecture]." Tile roofs also offered significant insulation, and the pitched attic spaces conveniently housed the newer buildings' larger mechanical and electrical equipment.

The firm frequently adopted a large-scale planning *parti* loosely identified as a quad, as in its library complex and dormitory buildings. Few

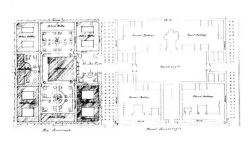

Plan of Bakewell and Brown's New Quadrangle (1916)

of the firm's buildings, however, had the architectural distinction of the original Richardsonian Romanesque structures. Beaux Arts-trained Bakewell and Arthur Brown Jr. designed buildings that were monumental and more ornate, more inflated in scale and in massing than the original, powerfully austere, and stylistically unified quad buildings. Nevertheless, the firm's work was sympathetic to the monumentality Stanford so desired and contributed significant additions to the campus's architecture with both structural and architectural innovations.

In the 1910s and 1920s, the university developed plans with Bakewell and Brown for new library and science quads to be located to the east and west respectively of the Inner Quad along its cross axis. Only the library quad was begun (the science quad waited until the 1950s), but it adequately demonstrated the difficulties encountered in building such large architectural units: at the time the university lacked sufficient resources to build a complete quad as well as the additional academic programs necessary to fill such large blocks of buildings. Although the library quad was blocked out in drawings, it was never entirely realized. The university could find funding for only a fraction of it, resulting in piecemeal construction over decades with various interpretations of the Spanish Mission style. The architecture lacked stylistic uniformity, and, ironically, isolated buildings again sprang up in this area of the campus, giving little sense of the intended harmony. With the onset of the Great Depression in the 1930s, increasing frugality and practicality further weakened the feasibility of complete quads. In fact, the quads envisioned by Bakewell and Brown were really large, formalized Beaux Arts precincts rather than replicas of the Inner Quad.

Some of Bakewell and Brown's proposals would have erased significant features of Olmsted's campus plan. In the 1910s Bakewell and Brown recommended an abstract Beaux Arts landscape around the Main Quad to harmonize it with the firm's new library quad. Its most significant feature called for the redesign of the Oval into a formalized garden based on axes and cross axes and central, circular courts. Although the plan was not realized, Bakewell and Brown's proposal to reinforce certain street axes with rows of trees, as on eastern campuses, found partial realization along Lasuen Street.

Cecil H. Green Library, Bing Wing

24. Cecil H. Green Library (formerly University Library)

Bing Wing (west wing)
> *Bakewell and Brown, 1919; The Architects Collaborative and Fields and Devereux, major restoration, 1995–1999*

East Wing *Hellmuth, Obata and Kassabaum, 1980*

With the destruction of the university's library building in the 1906 earthquake, the pressure for a more commodious facility grew increasingly sharp. Gradually, with most of the earthquake damage repaired, the university engaged Bakewell and Brown to prepare plans for a new library. Planned for the center of a vast new library quad (which eventually included the Art Gallery, the Hoover Library, and the Education Building), the library was sited at the end of an arcaded courtyard terminating the Inner Quad's axis to the east. (Olmsted's plan by contrast called for a string of open, interconnected quads). The plan was not fully realized, and the five-story library is perhaps more commanding than it might have been had the ensemble of surrounding single-story buildings and adjacent courtyards been built.

The architects stated that their large library building preserved the transverse axis of the quad by terminating its vista as Memorial Church terminated the main axis along Palm Drive. Its scale, according to the architects, was determined by these flanking low-rise buildings, which necessitated a large central mass to relieve the monotony of long rows of lower structures. The success of the plan, however, depended on its completion. Bakewell and Brown nevertheless seem to have intended a loose stylistic harmony to "give interest and variety to the whole group."

The heavy, buff-colored sandstone building is a typical Beaux Arts composition, consisting of a taller, dominant central block with lower flanking wings and a long, tall section for the stacks toward the south. It combines a stylistic blend of pseudo-Spanish, Gothic, and Mission details, such as figural sculpture, massive buttresses (originally meant to be crowned with sculpture), an arcade along the front, round-headed windows, and red-tile roofs. The large mass of the building, according to the architects, was broken up by projecting the central portion out over the arcades and by constructing low arcades on either side of it. The large arched windows and heavy buttresses introduce light and shade and reinforce the massiveness of the central part of the library. Although masonry construction is suggested, the building's main structural system is steel-frame, particularly evident in the broad window openings, although some areas of the structure incorporate hollow clay-tile walls and reinforced concrete.

The entrance lobby features a Beaux Arts ceremonial staircase leading to what was once the main reading room. The second lobby level is distinguished by an airy rotunda whose dome stands on a ring of foliated, slender columns. The *parti* of a central staircase rising into the main lobby with flanking corridors is strikingly reminiscent of George Kelham's San Francisco Public Library (1916). The plain, abstract detailing of wall surfaces as contrasting pure geometric shapes of solids and voids and the hierarchic massing of spaces punctuated by austere arches, window openings, and domed illumination, which draw one through the connecting rooms, were dramatic conventions used by the firm in many of their Stanford buildings. They used these devices elsewhere, such as Temple Emanu-El in San Francisco (1926) to heighten the old world ambiance.

The entire building was upgraded and seismically strengthened after sustaining severe damage in the 1989 earthquake. Renamed the Bing Wing to honor donors Peter and Helen Bing, its design has been carefully restored to Bakewell and Brown's original character.

25. Thomas Welton Stanford Art Gallery

Bakewell and Brown, 1917

The Art Gallery was built both to house a collection of paintings donated by Leland Stanford's brother and to create a stronger cultural presence closer to the Main Quadrangle than the Leland Stanford Junior Museum, which by 1917 had become something of a forlorn institution, stemming from curators' neglect and damage remaining from the 1906 earthquake. The Art Gallery also presented changing exhibitions. It was to anchor the northwest

Thomas Welton Stanford Art Gallery

corner of the new library quad. Although conceived virtually at the same time, the gallery is distinct in style from the library and, in fact, closer in design to the Richardsonian Romanesque quad. It is built of rough-faced sandstone veneer on concrete with a steel-truss, red-tile roof over a north-facing arcade. The gallery, however, is more overtly medieval than Spanish colonial, as is indicated by its cloisterlike columns and Moorish, interlaced arch-ribs of the plaster dome in the interior lobby. The exterior offers an exuberant contrast to the austere Richardsonian buildings, with more elaborate details, noticeably in the intricately carved moldings over the main entrance arch, as well as the tall, ornate, engaged columns surmounted by pinecones along the side. The curving corner and pronounced elevation copy the high base of the Outer Quad buildings, creating a visual tie with the older quad.

26. Education Building

Bakewell and Brown with Ellwood Cubberley, 1937–1938; Page and Turnbull, renovation, 1997

Education Building

The Education Building was sited along the western flank of the library quad as a three-story block. Its severely plain facade is distinctive of depression era architecture, with its Spanish-Mission details stripped down and abstracted, as in the heavy front buttresses and arcade. Wall surfaces are left clean, accenting the pure geometric shapes of the four great and two minor arches fronting a higher rectangular mass. As in most other Bakewell and Brown buildings, the materials suggest a smooth, ashlar-masonry construction in contrast to the rough-faced blocks of the Richardsonian Romanesque quad. The building has an underlying steel frame, evident in the extended spacing and size of the large, rectangular windows of the upper floor library. The building's function is symbolically represented by the names of famous educators scored into its upper walls, a conventional Beaux Arts touch, with Europeans and Americans listed separately.

The lobby, with its hexagonal tiled floor and heavy beam ceiling, features two mosaic vedutti scenes by Roccheggiani, a gift of Mrs. Timothy Hopkins, and leads to a main auditorium. On the second floor is the airy library, twenty-one feet high, with its mezzanine of metal stacks.

27. Hoover Tower *Arthur Brown Jr. with Bakewell and Weihe, 1938–1941*

Hoover Tower

In 1930 the Hoover War Library was to be a modest addition to the center of the north range of the library quad; it was to be linked in both style and theme to a War Memorial Building and Food Research Institute. The grouping was later dispersed, though the relationship between the Hoover Library and the war memorial was maintained; they were sited directly opposite each other across a fountain, clearly breaking with the planning tradition of the quad. Bakewell and Brown's monumental Hoover Tower is a singular structure topped at its 285-foot height by a carillon. President Wilbur claimed that it replaced Memorial Arch and the belfry of Memorial Church, both lost in the 1906 quake, as an architectural focal point. It was modeled after those from the cathedrals in Salamanca (like that which once rose over Memorial Church) and Mexico City. This relationship was more obvious in the published preliminary study for a squatter, heavier tower crowned by a shallow-pitched, red-tile roof rather than the present dome set over a tall observation deck. As constructed, it is immediately reminiscent of Bertram Goodhue's Nebraska State Capitol (1919–32) in Lincoln. Although the building is typical of the depression era's public works architecture, one wonders if the historical paring away may not have been the influence of Hoover himself, as in the ambiguous style of the Hoover house.

Hoover Tower is typical of Bakewell and Brown's blend of modern and historic elements: an uncompromising, hard-edged, smooth-faced shaft with slender, arcuated piers rising over a central block to an polygonal drum and red-tiled dome—a grander version of the firm's earlier use of towers at Stanford, as in the Old Union and Toyon Hall. The plain inset arch over columns distinguished the entrance, and leads to an unexpectedly grand lobby with four giant hybrid columns. To the east are additional Hoover structures: the Lou Henry Hoover Building (Charles Luckman Associates, 1967) and the Herbert Hoover Memorial Building (Sprankle, Lund and Sprague; Ernest J. Kump Associates, 1978), two three-story glass boxes concealed behind articulated concrete screens joined by a below-grade level. A single-story woodsy exhibition pavilion with exposed beams and trellises is squeezed between the two larger buildings on a platform that landscape architect Thomas Church tied into the base of the Hoover Tower in an attempt to create a single unit of buildings.

28. Memorial Hall *Bakewell and Brown, 1934, built 1936–1937; Sebastian and Associates, exterior modifications, 1997*

Memorial Hall

A memorial hall commemorating those from Stanford who died in World War I was planned shortly after the end of the war. Originally meant to be a part of the Hoover War Library in the library quad, it was finally established opposite the Hoover Tower. Various proposals for the design of the Memorial Hall included a large forecourt with enclosing wings leading past an entry exedra with a commemorative statue into a formal hall and auditorium. The hall was to be an imposing structure with a ground-floor colonnade and inscriptions and wreaths along the front facade, though the colonnade was deleted when the hall was finally built.

The spartan elevations and the cubic proportions of the building characterize Bakewell and Brown's work of the 1930s and the Depression era in general. The few Mission-style details are thoroughly abstracted into the most generic elements, covered colonnades along the sides, thick corner buttresses, bare wall surfaces punctuated with small openings, and a shallow red-tile roof. An oversized central arched entry, a faint reminder of the earlier exedra and the quad arcades, leads into the barrel-vaulted lobby, beyond which is the university's main auditorium. Appended to the rear of the building is space for Pigott Theater and the drama department. A new entry stair, terrace, and accessibility ramp were added in 1997, which bring some needed dimension to the main façade.

29. Harris J. Ryan Laboratory

Bakewell and Brown, 1926; Spencer and Ambrose, remodeling,
1958; demolished, 1988

The Ryan lab initially conducted high-voltage research. It was remodeled in
the 1950s for the study of nuclear power. It was demolished to make way
for faculty housing.

30. Press Building and Thomas M. Storke Student Publications Building

Press Building *1917, architect unknown; addition Bakewell and Brown, 1930;*
demolished 2000
Storke Student Publications Building *Hervey Parke Clark, 1964*

The original press building and its appendage are located in the area of the
current engineering complex to the south of the Main Quad. The Press
Building completed Bakewell and Brown's additions to the original plant
buildings behind the Main Quad. The warehouse portion of the building
was demolished to make way for the Mechanical Engineering Research
Laboratory (MERL) (#151).

31. Encina Gymnasium, Burnham Pavilion, DAPER Administration, and Roble Gymnasium

Encina Gymnasium *Bakewell and Brown, 1915; 1925; demolished, 2004*
Burnham Pavilion *Bakewell and Brown, 1921–1922; renovated, ELS Architects,*
1989–1990
DAPER Administration *Bakewell and Brown, 1927*
Roble Gymnasium *Bakewell and Brown, 1931*

Encina Gymnasium

Shortly before Encina Gymnasium's
construction, proposals were floated to
build an impressive physical education
and athletics complex on the site of the
demolished library and gymnasium
along Palm Drive. These plans were
scaled back, and more modest brick
buildings, the Encina Gymnasium, the
Stanford Pavilion for basketball (now
Burnham Pavilion), and the Board of
Athletic Control (BAC) administration
building (later known as the
Department of Athletics, Physical

Roble Gymnasium

Education, and Recreation or DAPER building) were built instead at a distance to the east. The buildings' chief interest is the use of brick as the major wall material, unique at Stanford; and the complementary siting, which once surrounded the Encina (men's) swimming pool and now encloses the Ford Quad, a handsome landscape area.

Most interesting of these buildings is Roble Gymnasium, located southwest of the Main Quad. Perhaps because it was designed for women, it is a more elegant structure with a domed lobby entered through coupled trefoil arches surmounted by a large quatrefoil window. The lobby itself is a cool cavern covered with a groin vault and decorative polygonal columns. Beyond, a colonnade of severe, polygonal-shaped Doric monoliths screen an internal courtyard, lending an almost Pompeian, atriumlike feel to the space. Large gym spaces open onto the court.

32. Stanford Stadium

Charles B. Wing, 1921; modifications 1925, 1927, 1960, 1994, and 1997

Stanford's most spectacular athletic structure is its stadium. Discussions for a "dirt stadium" were begun in 1914 with the Olmsted brothers and several sites were proposed, including the foothills and the demolished library and gymnasium area east of the Oval. The stadium, based on that of the ancient city of Pompeii, was sited on the northern edge of the campus

Stanford Stadium

and originally seated 60,000 spectators; at the time it was the second largest stadium in the United States after Yale's 75,000-seat facility.

The stadium was designed and constructed in less than nine months. Funded largely by alumni subscriptions, it was completed in time for the Stanford-Cal "Big Game" in 1921 (Stanford raced to complete its stadium before that rival institution could finish its own, in 1923). The earth from the bowl, which is 360 feet wide by 540 feet long and sunk 37 feet below grade, was used to build the encircling embankment 36 feet high. The oval was left open along the southeast, where an entry ramp led down into the bowl; there a stage for theatrical performances was located. John McLaren, superintendent of San Francisco's Golden Gate Park, designed the landscape of trees and shrubs on the stadium's outer slope. The stadium was enlarged in 1925 and again in 1927 to seat more than 85,000. Two concrete tunnels were added in 1973 to ease access and egress, but these removed some 800 seats. A press box was added in 1960 (expanded in 1994) and an all-weather track in 1978. A further upgrade in 1997 added an elevator, which was designed by Frederick Fisher and Partners with Heery International.

33. Old Union

Clubhouses *Charles Whittlesey, 1909–1915*
Arcaded Court and Central Building *Bakewell and Brown, 1922*

Old Union, 1922

The Stanford Union was the social center of the university until the construction of Tresidder Union in the 1960s. The old band pavilion originally occupied the site, where concerts and outdoor commencement ceremonies were held. Herbert Hoover, who in 1909 presented a scheme for bringing students, faculty, and alumni together on some common ground, promoted a student union. The Union building (men's clubhouse at the north side of the Union courtyard) was modeled after that at Harvard and included a dining hall, a library, a billiard room, a clothing store, and a smoke shop.

A clubhouse for women was built to the south to serve their various organizations and social events, since membership in the Stanford Union was then restricted to men. Although the original plan called for a connecting arcade and a third building (to the west) between the two clubhouses, only the two clubhouses were completed and opened in 1915. Bakewell and Brown added the remaining ingredients of the quad in 1922—a handsome, if formal Mission style building and an enclosing arcade marked by a grand entry flanked by Roman Doric columns and giant scrolls. Framed by domed bell towers, the building is graced with swan's neck arches set on columns over the main entry and includes Spanish colonial details such as wrought iron railings, decorative wall buttresses, and a quaint quatrefoil window immediately below the roof. The courtyard has a cloister's atmosphere, rather than an institutional feel, because it is secluded by the arcades and refreshed by a splashing fountain.

In the early 1960s, a student activities center and a new union, built in honor of President Donald Tresidder, replaced the older facilities. The main building was closed in 1965 and renovated the following year by Milton Pflueger, who converted it for administrative activities.

34. Carnegie Institution and Department of Plant Biology Addition, 280 Panama

Carnegie Institution *Bakewell and Brown, 1929*
Department of Plant Biology Addition *McLellan & Copenhagen, 1991*

This simple two-story and basement Beaux Arts building with a cast stone molding around the entrance arch is evocative of other campus buildings designed by Bakewell and Brown. The Carnegie Institution of Washington, D.C., operates research programs from this group of structures, with the participation of Stanford faculty and researchers.

35. Frost Amphitheater *Leslie Kiler, landscape architect, 1937*

A twenty-acre earthen bowl, the amphitheater was a gift of Mr. and Mrs. Howard Frost, as a memorial to their Stanford student son, John Laurence Frost.

Housing

With rising student enrollment through the 1920s and 1930s, existing dorms became overcrowded, promoting near riots in Encina. Presiding over the construction of several new dormitories during the 1910s–1930s, President Wilbur reaffirmed the university's ambition to house all undergraduate students on campus. Dorms were valued as important social tools for inculcating camaraderie, cooperation, and democratic principles; and the design of residence halls during these years endeavored to realize these ideals. The university abandoned the costly, difficult-to-manage hotel-like dorms, such as Encina, and instead built housing blocks broken into compact units of thirty to fifty students, somewhat as Olmsted had originally proposed in his "cottage system."

The university's desire to have faculty live on campus had met with mixed reactions before 1906: many faculty preferred to live in nearby Palo Alto, where they could purchase land rather than merely lease it. Eventually, however, several new subdivisions were opened, which added to the earliest faculty housing, located immediately south of the quad along Alvarado Row, Mayfield Avenue, and Lasuen Streets. The appeal of these new housing plats was their location: in the mid-1900s, the university opened up a subdivision in the hilly area south of Mayfield known as San Juan Hill (named by President Jordan after the Mission San Juan Capistrano, which he had visited and believed was the source of inspiration for the quad's architecture). This area continued to be developed into the 1940s.

The sampling of houses included in this walk represents the diversity of styles in vogue after the 1906 quake and prior to World War II. They include styles popular nationally, such as shingle, English Tudor, and Norman, as well as classic West Coast developments, such as Churrigueresque, Spanish colonial, and early Bay Area modernism. The adobe-like Hoover House is the gem of the San Juan Hill subdivision, though scattered around it are notable examples of local domestic architecture by Arthur Clark, Bakewell and Brown, John K. Branner (son of university president), and Charles Sumner, among others.

With the exception of Frank Lloyd Wright's radical Hanna House, located on the fringes of the San Juan Hill subdivision, faculty residences seem to express the provincial nature of Stanford as a regional university. (It is interesting to note the sharp contrast between the housing styles before and after World War II: with the rise of science and technology, and the recognition of Stanford as an international university, its residential architecture, particularly the modern Bay Area style, invariably featured idioms influenced by international developments.)

36. Toyon Hall and Branner Hall *1923*

Toyon and Branner Halls were to form the nucleus of a much larger student housing quad immediately behind Encina Hall. Indicative of Stanford's origins and the firm's penchant for Beaux Arts planning, the quad was organized on a system of axes and cross axes punctuated by public nodes. The grouping of two- and three-story, nearly identical housing units around courtyards retained the Main Quad's qualities of enclosure and architectural unity, if not its actual form. This concept was completed with Kimball Hall (1991), Lantana

and Castaño Hall (1992), and the Schwab Residential Center (1997). Toyon, which originally housed 150 men, is screened by a colonnaded passageway opening onto a landscaped courtyard entrance framed by Mission-style residence halls marked at their corners by open towers. Inside, a restrained, Spanish colonial–detailed assembly hall joins the two L-shaped wings in which each floor had fifteen suites, consisting of a bedroom and a study shared by two students, and a communal lounge and bathroom as well as a sleeping porch. Branner is marked by a central lounge joining three similar wings around a central court, which is flanked by a high-ceilinged dining hall. The dining hall is similar to the one at Lagunita Court.

37. Lagunita Court

Arthur Brown Jr., and Bakewell and Weihe, 1934; additions 1937; renovations and additions to dining hall, Gordon Chong and Partners, 1998

Branner Hall, 1923

Lagunita Court, 1935

Lagunita Court was built to house the increased enrollment of women following the university's decision in 1933 to rescind its policy of limiting the admission of women to five hundred (which Jane Stanford established in 1899). Like Toyon, Lagunita Court is based on a "house" system organized into a symmetrical composition of long, connecting, parallel wings joined by the dining hall to form an enclosed court around a large landscaped courtyard. The six independent two-story buildings each held 39 students in one- and two-student occupancy rooms with shared dining, laundry, and social facilities. A few years later, wings were added on either side of the rear pavilions, providing housing for 80 students in each wing.

The Spanish Mission style buildings were hailed for their pioneering lightweight steel frames. Stanford faculty members J. B. Wells and A. S. Niles engineered the structure, using the Soule Steel Company's Unibuilt steel frame construction technique. The frame was arc-welded and

OPPOSITE: *Toyon Hall*

Lagunita Dining Hall, 1935

consisted of six-inch-deep, open-web studs prefabricated into panels that were shipped to the site and hoisted onto a prepared concrete foundation. Bakewell and Brown's fondness for marrying historicism with modern technology is especially evident here in the dining hall, with its exposed wood roof and wooden paneling, masking the underlying steel frame. The stripped-down walls and repetitive, simple, large abstract forms, however, are appropriate expressions of the steel frame.

38. Roble Hall and Ventura Hall

Roble Hall   *George Kelham, 1918*
Ventura Hall   *Bakewell and Brown, 1926*

Roble Hall, 1919

While Bakewell and Brown were engaged in designing many buildings for the university at this period, George Kelham was hired to build a new women's dorm to replace the original Roble Hall, which was converted into a men's dorm and renamed Sequoia Hall. Long thought to have been built of reinforced concrete, its buff-colored walls are actually hollow clay tiles. Roble is an elegant, Spanish eclectic style buildings with a red-tile roof embellished with decorative pilaster panels flanking the ground floor's round-headed windows, iron railings supported by carved brackets, and a freestanding classical portico surmounted by a balcony over the main entry. The large round-headed windows along the end of the main elevations, which now serve as fire escapes, feature figural panels in their pediments and in their sill panels. Fortunately it was seismically upgraded in 1988, just in time for the Loma Prieta earthquake in 1989.

Kelham, who designed the San Francisco Public Library (1916), conceived Roble as two H-plans side by side, but only one block and an additional wing were built and joined by what was to be a temporary hall. Roble's three stories housed two-hundred women in separate rooms, some sharing sitting rooms, which were broken up into units of fifty in each wing, one floor of the center arm, and an additional wing. Two dining rooms were included in the main building. The refinement of Roble Hall, in contrast to the heavy forms and abstract details of Bakewell and Brown's men's dorms, may reflect Kelham's experience designing the Palace Hotel in San Francisco.

Ventura Hall, a California Spanish style building, was originally built at 344 Serra Street as an apartment house for bachelor professors. The building was remodeled in 1938 as a women's dormitory. In 1940 "Casita Annex," with space for an additional twenty students, was created by reconstructing the adjacent garage. Ventura housed women students until 1961 when it was converted to administrative space and the Institute for Mathematical Studies in the Social Sciences located its office in the structure. During seven days between August 23 and August 30, 1982, the complex was cut into sections and moved to its current location at the crossroads of Campus Drive and Panama Street and reassembled in slightly different configuration. The building now houses the Center for the Study of Language and Information.

39. Bechtel International Center (formerly Zeta Psi Fraternity)

John K. Branner, 1917; remodeled 1963; additions, Hawley and Peterson, 1978

The I-Center, an information and social center for international students at Stanford, was originally a fraternity house. Previously housed in the Inner Quad and then in a house on Lasuen Street that was destroyed by fire in 1961, the International Center moved in 1963 to this house, which was remodeled with the sponsorship of the Bechtel Corporation.

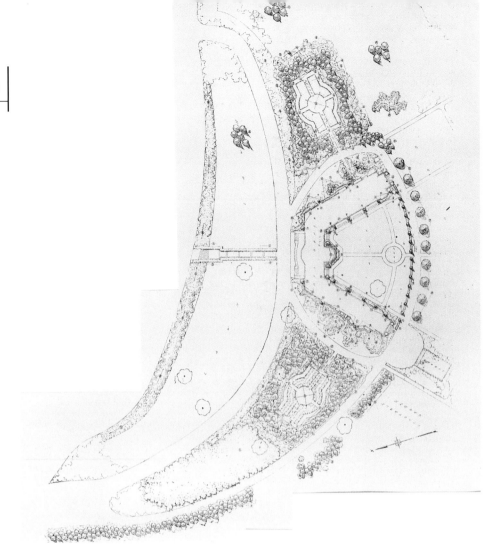

Mr. McLaren's Plan for the President's Hill

40. The Knoll (formerly the President's House)

Louis Christian Mullgardt, 1918

After President Ray Lyman Wilbur had rejected several sites, the university trustees accepted his recommendation to locate the house at the head of the main axis of Palm Drive, where the Stanfords had initially considered placing their mausoleum. (A good view of the house and its relation to Palm Drive can be had from the observation deck of Hoover Tower.) The site was once known as Cemetery Hill, a graveyard dating before the university. In 1908 after a student prank exposed a grave, the cemetery was moved to allow for future development.

Mullgardt, a draftsman for Shepley, Rutan, and Coolidge before he relocated to California in 1905, was best known at the time for his Court of Ages in the San Diego Panama-California Exposition (1915) and the M. H. de Young Memorial Museum in Golden Gate park (1916). The Knoll reflects his taste for the extremely ornate variation of the Spanish colonial style known

The Knoll, 1918

as Churrigueresque, which the architect had helped to popularize in the San Diego exposition.

The house's unusual form—a butterfly plan with canted wings—spreads over the hilltop with its commanding views while enclosing a south-facing garden. The walls are plastered in pink stucco that is combed. Constructed of reinforced concrete, the large scale of the house was dictated by the need for a university reception center. The three floors wedge into the slope of the hill, with servants occupying the ground floor, and the family's living and bedrooms and guest quarters on the upper floors. Mullgardt also designed the interiors and their furnishings.

The interiors were modified to meet the needs of various academic purposes after the Wilburs moved out in 1943, including being used as the home of the music department (until the Braun Music building was built) and since 1986, the Center for Computer Research in Music and Acoustics (CCRMA). In 2005, the Knoll is undergoing major renovation to address seismic problems and to accommodate the technical and performance needs of CCRMA.

41. Atalaya, Meyer Buck Estate

Arthur Brown Jr., 1918; renovations, Page & Turnbull, 2002–2003

Atalaya, 1919

J. Henry Meyer commissioned Brown to design a second Atalaya (the Spanish word for "watchtower," a feature of Meyer's first house, which was destroyed by fire) in a French Mediterranean inspired house. Cream-colored stucco walls punctuated by square-headed windows with wrought-iron balcony railings distinguish the two-story house. A hipped, red-tile roof is set behind a concrete balustrade. Meyer's daughters, Alice Meyer Buck and Eugenie Olga Meyer, bequeathed the house to Stanford University in 1979, which used it as a campus conference facility until being closed in the early 1990s. Recently, the house has been extensively renovated and now is the home for the Stanford Provost. In addition, the William R. Hewlett Foundation leased a portion of the estate and has constructed its headquarters building here.

42. Kingscote Gardens, *1917*

Kingscote was built for Mrs. Burt Estes Howard, widow of a faculty member, who wanted to provide rental housing on campus for faculty. The four-story apartment building offers a restrained Arts and Craft atmosphere on a secluded landscaped garden site.

43. Hoover House, Stanford University President's House

> *Arthur and Birge Clark, architects, with Lou Henry Hoover, 1919; Thomas Church, landscape architect, 1950s*

U.S. President Herbert Hoover and his wife, Lou Henry Hoover, had lived on campus in various rentals for a number of years before deciding to build their own house in 1917. Lou Henry (Mrs. Herbert) Hoover oversaw the design while her husband was in Paris, and greatly influenced its outcome. The Hoovers' first choice of an architect, Louis Mullgardt, who was completing the president's house on campus, the Knoll, was soon dismissed after he had announced the commission, though it seems more likely that his preliminary design, which resembled the flamboyant Spanish baroque of the Knoll, was distasteful to the modest Hoovers. (Mullgardt had earlier designed posters for Herbert Hoover's Belgian Relief Fund.) The Hoovers then turned

to local architect Arthur Clark, who taught architectural drafting and drawing at the university, and who was assisted by his son, Birge Clark, a recent graduate of Columbia University's architecture program.

Sited on the steep slope of San Juan Hill, the house gently angles around the curve of the hill in an irregular composition of stacked, white-washed cubes, and flat roofs suggest a Mediterranean or Algerian hilltown, places, in fact, that Lou Hoover may have visited and recommended that her architect emulate. The abstract, sculptural qualities of the design are heightened by such rich details as an exterior staircase set behind a stepped wall zigzagging to the roof (a motif found in Pueblo pottery to represent clouds); a corbelled balcony over a broad-arched, deeply recessed entry; thick reveals around simple wall openings and straight-headed windows; and articulated chimney tops.

Outdoor living is fundamental to the design: the irregular silhouette of the roofs was intended to hide a pool and a tennis court, neither of which was realized, and terraces and patios extend the indoor living spaces through broad, glazed openings to make the landscaped surroundings an integral part of the design. The house's sprawling composition, openness, and flexibility embody Lou Hoover's desire that "our house...be an elastic thing, never entirely finished, always growing with the needs of our family and be adaptable to our changing needs."

The house has been described variously as Pueblo or Hopi Indian and Spanish colonial, though neither appellation is completely appropriate. The house is a remarkably modern design, largely free of the historical precedents associated with those styles. Its closest precedent, geographically and stylistically, seems to be Irving Gill's contemporaneous pared down Spanish colonial concrete houses in Southern California, though Birge Clark claimed not to have been aware of this work. However, Gill's buildings and essays appeared often in such journals as the *Architect and Engineer* and *The Craftsman,* both of which were accessible to the architects. In fact, Gill's seminal essay, "The Home of the Future—The New Architecture of the West" appeared in both journals in 1916. Using both reinforced concrete and brick walls that have been plastered over, the building's informal quality of the Pueblo architecture, as Gill discovered, has been filtered through a hard-edged, pure geometric aesthetic giving a surprising modern look.

The exterior masks a more conventional interior; the rooms are formal spaces, lined with dark wood paneling uncharacteristic of the pueblo like style of the house's exterior. Hoover furnished the house with Mexican and native American Indian pottery and rugs, suggesting a closer, conscious affinity with the Pueblo tradition than the architects admitted. Chrysanthemums, emblem of the Geological and Mining Society of

OPPOSITE: *Hoover House, 1920*

American Engineers, of which both Hoovers were members (Lou Henry Hoover was the first woman to receive a degree from the Geology Department at Stanford), adorned the entrance hall, where its patterns decorated one wall. In 1945, Herbert Hoover donated the house to the university for use as the president's residence, superseding the Knoll.

The Hoover House is a National Historic Landmark

44. Paul and Jean Hanna House, 737 Frenchman's Road

Frank Lloyd Wright, 1936–1960; Architectural Resources Group, restoration, 1997–1999

The Hanna House marked a watershed in Wright's career; it was his first design to be built using the unconventional geometry of the hexagon. Wright's choice of the form was intended to be both witty and functional. Educators Paul and Jean Hanna commissioned a house that would grow and change with their family, and Wright obliged, believing that the hexagon's 180-degree reflex angles permitted greater "to and fro" than the conventional right angle. Wright's solution also satisfied the Hannas' wish that their children grow up in an environment receptive to Dewey-inspired educational principles of learning by doing (a large playroom forms an intimate part of the living-dining areas).

Hanna House, 1957

The Hanna house is generally considered a prototypical Usonian, a term coined by Wright to identify the United States. The Usonian was a moderate-cost, mass-produced suburban type that Wright developed in the 1930s, consisting of a kit-of-parts assembled on a concrete mat, its prefab walls raised and positioned on a geometric module scored into a radiant-heated floor. Wright devised an original method of prefabricated "sand-wich" walls: boards and battens screwed back to back into studs, creating an insulation-lined inner pocket between the outer and inner walls, which were erected simultaneously. The thin, yet structurally strong walls were fit-ted into brass boots embedded in the floor. In the 1950s, when the Hannas reconfigured the interiors after their children had moved away, they said the process was a simple matter of screwing and unscrewing the walls.

The great flexibility of the Usonian enabled the Hannas to recon-figure the playroom into a large dining room, the children's bedrooms into a master bedroom and bath, and the study and old master bedroom into a large study with fireplace. Unlike the prototypical Usonian, the Hanna house used central rather than radiant heating and occupied a large lot on an exposed foothill rather than a confined suburban tract. Wright's prefab walls were actually constructed by local carpenters onsite.

The house is poised dramatically around the brow of the hill and climbs its way around it in angular shifts leading to the guest room and hobby shop. From the base of the hill off of Frenchman's Road the house is approached from an oblique angle, offering ever-changing glimpses of its main elevation from below. Passing under the deep, dark, low-lying overhang of the carport (possibly a Wright innovation) and through the narrow doorway leading into the hexagonal, double-height, skylit vestibule, the visitor experiences the contrasting psychological effects of Wright's spaces: informal and formal, broad and narrow, low and high, dark and light, confinement and release. Passage through the house forms a hexagonal route around the massive sunken hearth and the attached central spine of the kitchen. The angular shifts define a distinct spatial and functional area, so that each retains its requisite privacy without impeding the continuity and fluidity of the whole. From within, the house seems to extend physically and visually in every direction, an effect accented by the thin, shoji-like window walls, many of which open onto outdoor terraces. Visual terminal points evaporate in a haze of light.

The gardens grew piecemeal. The site featured an oak and cypress, which were incorporated into the design of the house. Wright also planned a row of tall conifers along the rear of the property, but the Hannas rejected this idea, fearing that their view of the foothills would be lost. In 1952 they added a curving drive along the front of the house for which Wright designed the extensive retaining wall. And the cascading pool and summerhouse were added after Wright's death in 1960, designed by William Wesley Peters, his principal assistant at Taliesin. The cascade waterfall was inspired by Wright's Fallingwater, which the Hannas had visited. Also in the 1960s the Hannas incorporated a two-tone urn next to the drive from the Imperial Hotel in Tokyo, also designed by Wright in the late 1910s and made from oya-lava stone.

In 1975, the Hannas gave the house to the university, and it served as the provost's residence until 1989, when it was severely damaged in the Loma Prieta earthquake. Engineers discovered that soil improperly compacted when the house was built was causing the main fireplace and related walls near it to shift. The house has been restored and seismically upgraded and reopened in April 1999 as a conference and reception facility for Stanford.

The Hanna House is a National Historic Landmark

45. Faculty Houses – Santa Ynez, Gerona Avenue, Mirada Avenue, and Salvatierra Street

Mazour House, 781 Frenchman's Road *Ernest Born, 1947.* The vertical board-and-batten siding, sloping flat roofs over clerestories, and closed front elevation make this house a distinctive example of the Bay Area style popularized by William Wurster and other architects. Faculty houses of interest include:

747 Santa Ynez, Hempl House *John Bakewell Jr., 1909*

767 Santa Ynez (now 618 Mirada), Arthur Clark House *Arthur Clark, 1909*

770 Santa Ynez, Martin House *Birge Clark, 1926*, a Tudor revival house

774 Santa Ynez *Arthur Clark, 1909*

775 Santa Ynez, McFarland House *Arthur Clark, 1910*, which Clark considered to be his finest

536 Gerona, Craig House *Charles Sumner, 1929*

540 Gerona, Weber House *Charles Sumner*

553 Gerona, Paul House *Aaron Green, 1939*. The architect, one of Frank Lloyd Wright's more talented apprentices, designed this low-slung house along hexagonal lines similar to the nearby Hanna House.

635 Gerona, Guerard House *John K. Branner, 1926*

692 Mirada, Wolter House *John K. Branner, 1926*

736 Mirada, Bunting House *Henry Gutterson*. Gutterson, a Beaux Arts trained architect, worked in the offices of Daniel Burnham, Willis Polk, and John Galen Howard.

El Escarpado *Charles Sumner, 1927*. Three houses designed as a unit in the English Tudor style and organized around a knoll overlooking Lake Lagunita.

625–627 Salvatierra Street, Double House for Board of Trustees
   Bakewell and Brown, 1906

635 Salvatierra Street *Charles Sumner*

707 Salvatierra Street, Erwin House *Charles Sumner, circa 1929*

708 Salvatierra Street, Merrill House *Charles Sumner, 1929*

711 Salvatierra Street, Hinsey House *Charles Sumner, 1930*

712 Salvatierra Street, Snodgrass House *Charles Sumner, 1929*

715 Salvatierra Street, Farnsworth House *Charles Sumner, 1930*

716 Salvatierra Street, Sellards House *John K. Branner, 1935*. The neoclassical entrance flanked by lower wings resembles the character of San Francisco architect William Wurster's work, all elegantly detailed.

PART FOUR

The Post-War Campus 1945–1980

57

62

61

54 53

52

51

47

46

8

50 49

65
64

58

N

Building the Post-War Campus

The brief presidency of Donald Tresidder (1943–1948) profoundly affected Stanford's architectural character and direction after World War II. In 1944, Lewis Mumford, one of America's foremost critics of modern culture, architecture, and urban planning, was hired as professor of humanities within Stanford's newly organized school of humanities, a position he occupied until 1945. (Mumford was introduced to the dean of the school by Paul Hanna, who had commissioned Frank Lloyd Wright to design the Hanna "Honeycomb" house in 1936.) Following Mumford's recommendation, Tresidder established the first university planning office. He named as its director (on a part-time basis of 80 hours a month) Eldridge T. Spencer, a Beaux Arts-trained San Francisco architect. Shortly after leaving Stanford, Mumford was invited to review the progress of the planning office and to draw up proposals for developing a master plan, including recommendations for its architectural character.

Mumford submitted his planning report in 1947. In it he praised Olmsted's original plan and hoped that a "concentrated urban group in a permanent rural setting" would be preserved through a surrounding green belt and the prohibition of cars from the heart of the campus. The green belt, the ring road or Campus Drive, was created primarily at Mumford's suggestion, though its nearly full realization waited until the 1970s. Mumford argued for separated modern buildings that were linked by covered walkways, based on a planning scheme he had seen at Reading University in England:

> I recommend that a fresh effort at unity in terms of our own day be made. The tie-in between the new and the old should be, first, with respect to height and scale, and second, in the use of the covered walk or arcade, the esthetic connecting thread between the individual buildings, and as a necessary functional adoption to circulation on foot.

Mumford's recommendation stemmed from his criticism of the original planning of the quad's arcades, which he believed resulted in "bad lighting, unnecessary noise, and a cramped ground plan." Mumford proposed that "by using the arcade as a free-standing spine, and designing the buildings in repetitive units at an angle to the arcade, an effective open plan can be created which will give a maximum of light, of accessibility, and of space for extension." Spencer also adopted Mumford's proposals in his master plans of 1948 and 1949 and therefore shunned Stanford's historic approach to planning around quads. Spencer attempted to abandon its most familiar architectural ingredients—the red-tile roof and arches—and instead opted for singularly modern buildings, typically long, one- or two-story concrete structure with flat roofs. The uncompromising rectilinear forms, blank walls juxtaposed with large areas of glass, covered walkways, and out-door patios, were features largely singled out by Mumford as "proper" to modern day circumstances.

Spencer mitigated the impact of his "contemporary" architecture by citing its economic and functional benefits. But when he unveiled his master plan in a controversial 1948 exhibition, "Stanford Builds," alumni in particular condemned the absence of familiar elements. Mumford himself also condemned the use of red-tile roofs, which he considered "obsolete" and even "dangerous." Tresidder supported Spencer's plans and Mumford's recommendations, calling for "new educational buildings [that] will not seek to imitate in steel and glass and concrete, the truly inimitable beauty of the stone-built quads. Such imitation can never succeed. Rather we shall build with today's materials, harmoniously, but as of the present." Spencer's dorm, Stern Hall (1947–48), became the center of rancorous debate about Stanford's architectural future. Its flat roofs and bare concrete walls prompted comparisons to industrial architecture. Stanford had entered the arena of modern architecture and planning.

John Carl Warnecke, an alumnus who had studied architecture at Harvard under Walter Gropius, one of the founders of the international style, was drawn into the debate, arguing for a middle ground. Warnecke proposed contextual buildings constructed in modern materials and retaining the traditional elements of sloping red-tile roofs; textured, buff-colored walls; and connecting arcades. These "emotional" features, he believed, were fundamental to the Stanford experience. Indeed, the irony of Spencer, a Beaux Arts graduate, arguing for truly modern architecture, and Warnecke, a student of Gropius's Bauhaus, choosing a less controversial path, is difficult to explain. Perhaps Spencer's experience with industrial architecture and low-cost housing projects led him to adopt a more modern aesthetic. Warnecke, who had also trained with his father and Arthur Brown, had come to embrace their attitudes of an architectural unity, especially by means of the red-tile roofs, as Bakewell and Brown had practiced.

Numerous national exhibitions were brought to the campus to pro-mote modern architecture. In 1946 Robert Anshen, best known for his case study house and his later work with Joseph Eichler, a popular and innovative tract house builder, lectured on the "Postwar House and its Materials," which accompanied an exhibition of the same title. In 1947 an exhibition of photographs of Frank Lloyd Wright's houses, including the Hanna House, opened. And in 1948 *Life* magazine's "Houses, U.S.A." followed Spencer's "Stanford Builds" exhibition. Yet Spencer's position was undermined by Frank Lloyd Wright in 1965, when he visited the campus and delivered a lecture condemning Stanford's recent architecture as a "confused mass of disassociated buildings in a bastard style of architecture," a pointed rebuke of the red-tile roofs and buff-colored structures loosely modeled after the original quad. Wright reserved his praise for the university's original buildings, the Inner Quad, which he felt revealed the "hand of the master," Henry Hobson Richardson.

Spencer nevertheless continued to introduce modern architecture to the Stanford campus, whether as director of planning, executive architect (with his firm of Spencer and Ambrose), or supervising architect. In 1957 he served as supervising architect of Gardner Dailey's physics buildings and Edward Durell Stone's Stanford University Hospital. Both buildings were quickly damned by "the Chief," Herbert Hoover, perhaps Stanford's most powerful alumnus, and eventually this led to Spencer's resignation in 1959.

Afterward the university no longer relied on a consulting campus architect to design most of its buildings, but instead hired independent firms. In 1961, these firms were selected with the recommendation of an advisory council including the architects John Carl Warnecke, Milton Pflueger, Gardner Dailey, and Ernest Kump, and the landscape architects Thomas Church and Robert Royston. Not surprisingly most of the major buildings and landscapes completed on the campus during the 1960s and 1970s fell to this group, as well as to Spencer's firm.

The Rise of Science and Technology, 1950s to 1970s

Stanford's newly opened Planning Office faced a daunting task: overseeing the development and planning of over 8,000 acres of university property, most of which was agricultural land, reflecting the institution's regional status. Initially university president Donald Tresidder and his successor, Wallace Sterling (1949–68), envisioned an expanded mission for the university, capitalizing on government-sponsored research in science and engineering. Stanford was determined not only to enter the atomic age, but also to lead it.

Much of Stanford's postwar construction was for engineering, science, and medicine. Academic leaders such as Frederick Terman pushed for the establishment of a new science and engineering quad and a light-industrial research park, the first of its kind associated with a university in the United States. But often, overall planning was opportunistic, reflecting the rapid emergence of new technologies and an intuitive development of research across a variety of scientific disciplines based on a cross-fertilization of ideas. In the 1960s these external events propelled Stanford to national prominence.

The university, eager to determine its planning options beyond those considered by Mumford and Spencer, solicited recommendations for the development of the its lands from Clarence Stein and Skidmore, Owings, and Merrill (1953), among others. Stein, one of the most influential twentieth-century urban planners in America, believed that Stanford had the "opportunity to create the first American contemporary city" with its population enjoying "a good life close to nature, and it is to be hoped, also close to work." Stein envisioned a city composed of such elements as "complete neighborhoods, green belts, dispersed industry, modern community and market centers ... that will be not only more sightly and more livable [than the contemporary metropolis] but more easy and less costly to operate."

Stein urged adopting a "comprehensive design embracing the site, the mass of buildings and their relation to each other and to the natural setting." In essence he envisioned a garden city, citing the models of the twelve New Towns in England, as well as Letchworth and Welwyn. At Stanford, he proposed to locate residential areas to "open on spacious views of old trees, great recreation areas or farms and distant hills. The city that is to be created," he further elaborated, "can be a truly green city, with gardens and peaceful, safe parks outside of everyone's door and with broad agricultural or natural green belts in easy walking distance. This is the kind of beautiful and healthful city that can be built at Stanford." Stein's proposals were viewed by many as too idyllic, providing no practical provisions for an industrial park or other commercial ventures.

In 1953 the university hired the architectural firm of Skidmore, Owings, and Merrill (SOM) to create a new master plan to develop and zone Stanford's lands for academic, residential, commercial, and light industrial uses, along with a system of circulation. SOM's plan, however, fell far short of Stanford's aspirations; most of the land was reserved for suburban development, allowing only a minimal presence for light industry and commerce. SOM projected that the university's profitable growth would stem from escalating land values for housing rather than industry or commerce. Dissatisfied with SOM's limited vision, the university reapportioned the acreage, allocating almost half of its 8,400 acres for academic, industrial, and commercial development, while holding the remainder as an academic reserve.

Two distinct yet corresponding areas of the campus were zoned for significant development: a science quad west of the Inner Quad and an industrial park on the eastern fringe of the campus. President Sterling imagined a unique pedagogic and research community based on a "cross fertilization" of ideas among "scientists in different fields required in modern science and technology." These included physicists, engineers, mathematicians, and geophysicists. The high energy physics lab (with its linear accelerator) opened the area west of the Main Quad for science in 1948, and a thirty-acre science quad followed in 1966. A new chemistry quad was located north of the science and engineering complex, which Spencer planned as a loosely organized quadrangular arrangement of buildings. A new medical center was sited nearby. None of the quads, however, ever fully materialized as planned; nor did the resultant buildings "harmonize with the 'Romanesque' of the main quad" and its landscaping, as Sterling had proposed. Herrin Hall and Labs, Mudd Chemistry Building, and the Varian complex are almost generic, modernist buff-painted reinforced concrete structures with partial red-tile roofs that mimic Stanford's earliest architecture.

Applied Electronics Laboratory

The Stanford Industrial Park (1951) —later renamed the Stanford Research Park—was more influential than the science quad in its planning and design. Zoning controls and planning guidelines encouraged a residential feel and style in design, with landscaping along deep front setbacks and concealed parking facilities, giving the impression of a residential enclave rather than an industrial park. The light-industrial nature of the earliest companies and their buildings required an unconventional typology for high-tech research and development that would lead to the corporate campus in the 1970s and 1980s. Some of these buildings were quite stunning and elegant variations of the industrial shed: the Hewlett-Packard buildings set obliquely to Page Mill combine polychromatic brick walls, rows of factory lights, and a fully glazed northern exposure, which, during the predawn hours, is spectacularly illuminated. Although mixed use development and increased traffic now affect the suburban qualities of the Stanford Research Park, as do some of the more recent large buildings which are overexposed to the street, it still remains a twentieth-century planning paradigm.

Record Growth

Stanford recorded unprecedented construction expenditures in the late 1940s and 1960s. In 1966 it reported its greatest building boom since its founding; a construction spurt heated by rapidly rising enrollment (doubling immediately after World War II to 8,000 students), housing demands, and the need to update academic facilities. By 1967 the board of trustees was allocating some 4,400 acres of land for academic purposes. By comparison, when the university opened in 1891, 440 acres was set aside for academic needs, though the buildings themselves occupied only 40 acres.

Stanford's budget for new buildings and renovations made huge leaps, reaching all-time highs in 1966 and 1973. The momentum was sustained by the "Plan of Action for a Challenging Era" (PACE), a fund-raising campaign announced by Stanford in 1961. The three-year $100 million drive was based on a $25 million three-for-one Ford Foundation challenge grant. In 1973 the university embarked on another building program whose objective was a "Dynamic Steady State," designed to consolidate departments while making the quad the focal point of campus academic life.

46. W. W. Hansen Laboratories (Microwave Lab and High Energy Physics Lab) and Ginzton Laboratory

W. W. Hansen Laboratories *Spencer & Ambrose, 1949–1954*
Ginzton Laboratory *Spencer & Ambrose, 1953; additions, 1956, 1959*

These are the only buildings remaining from Spencer's science quad. They are strongly reminiscent of Spencer's Stern Hall and their simple flat-roofed concrete block walls of one and two stories.

47. Physics Lecture Hall, Russell H. Varian Laboratory of Physics, and Jack A. McCullough Building

Physics Lecture Hall *Gardner Dailey, 1957; demolished 1997*

Russell H. Varian Laboratory of Physics *Gardner Dailey, 1963*

Jack A. McCullough Building *Gardner Dailey, 1965*

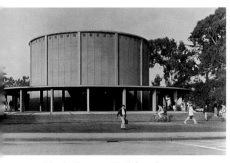

Physics Lecture Hall (1957)

A technology quad had been planned for this area under President Donald Tresidder as early as 1945. It was intended to bridge education and industry, as in the McCullough Building, which became a national center for space age material research where scientists and engineers shared labs, offices, and classrooms. Spencer initially proposed modern, low-rise buildings with flat roofs reminiscent of Stern Hall, much like his microwave laboratory (1949), one of the first buildings in the quad. Dailey, however, was later hired to design subsequent buildings, giving them a more monumental presence. His tripartite composition of buildings was to be erected in stages, and he was asked to compose as the centerpiece of this arrangement a strongly independent building that could stand by itself until the quad was complete in toto.

Dailey's Physics Lecture Hall, unaffectionately known as the Tank, sat behind a large fountain courtyard and a colonnade linking flanking buildings (the Varian and McCullough Buildings), somewhat reminiscent of the library quad. The lecture hall was a circular, concrete-frame building that never endeared itself to the Stanford community. Shortly after construction was begun, Herbert Hoover condemned it as uncharacteristic of the Stanford vernacular and an "eyesore until the University will some day need tear it down." (At the same time, however, he proposed a second Hoover Tower on the west side of the Main Quad!)

Hoover's concerns prompted the board of trustees to reissue its resolution that buildings erected near the quad "conform to the Romanesque form of architecture as modified in the original inner and Outer Quad, due allowance being made for modern costs and materials." Dailey and Spencer, who acted as the university's supervising architects, were branded as "contemporary flats," and the physics building was one in a string of controversial buildings that eventually led to Spencer's resignation in 1959.

Lomita Mall, originally landscaped by Thomas Church, fronts Dailey's tripartite composition and winds its way up to the Terman Engineering Building. With the demolition of the Physics Lecture Hall in 1997, the western axis from the Main Quad was reopened, and a new science and engineering quad has reshaped that architectural technological landscape.

48. William F. Durand Building and Hugh Hildreth Skilling Building *Spencer, Lee, and Busse, 1967–1969*

Durand Building

The Durand Building typifies the brutalist influence on much university architecture in the United States during the 1960s and 1970s, and on the Stanford campus it marks a dramatic departure from the more modest concrete buildings of Spencer's earlier work. The building shares stylistic features with Warnecke's contemporaneous Meyer Library, with its cantilevered roofs raised high on thin piers, indicating a certain uniformity of design encouraged by Stanford's Architects Advisory Council, formed after Spencer's resignation.

The four-story, buff-colored, concrete-frame structure is in fact a major and a minor block joined by encircling cantilevered balconies, which are interrupted over the main entries on the east and west elevations. The infill is aluminum and gray glass curtain wall. The concrete piers rise through the balconies to support a shallow-pitched, cantilevered mansard-style roof. The concrete surfaces are variously treated; for example, heavy sandblasting, rough, board-formed texture, and cement plaster. Although the detailing of the concrete is typical of the brutalist aesthetic, it also loosely suggests the rough-faced ashlar of the quad on the other side of the plaza. Following Stanford convention, the roof material is variegated red tile, and its form gives the building a strong horizontal emphasis.

Before its dedication, the structure was originally called the Space Engineering Building and housed interdisciplinary research in Stanford's aerospace program establish by Professor Durand, who developed the first variable pitch propeller, and fostered collaborative research into space age engineering and science among education, industry, and government.

49. Ruth Wattis Mitchell Earth Sciences Building

Spencer, Lee, and Busse, 1968–1970; David Bartlett & Associates, seismic renovation, 1997

Mitchell Earth Sciences

One of Spencer's more modest reinforced concrete and glass buildings, the Earth Sciences Building is stylistically similar to the much larger Durand building. The building sits in a sunken court, its skeletal frame rising through two balcony levels to support a broadly cantilevered red-tile roof set under a dark-tinted glazed upper story. The concrete surfaces show the imprint of both rough and smooth textured boards. The building's lobby has an unexpected accent: a glazed library court organized around a spiral staircase, perhaps inspired by Eero Saarinen's design at the General Motors Tech Center in Warren, Michigan.

50. Terman Engineering Center *Harry Weese Associates, 1974–1977*

The Terman Engineering Center reflects the 1970s interest in efficient, low-tech environmental systems. The L-shaped plan capitalizes on solar orientation and maximizes the number of outside windows. Skylights, bronze-tinted windows, balcony doors, and sliding wooden louvers all open, giving the impression of a lively residential rather than institutional community. This feeling is further enhanced inside the building where communal "streets" ring open courts. Louvered interior doors provide cross-ventilation, and vertical shafts bring light and air to all seven floors, including those below ground level. All floors open onto the reflecting pool and landscaped garden, which were redesigned by Peter Walker in the early 1990s. Modular offices have movable walls that can convert the spaces into larger seminar and conference rooms or even labs. Exposed ducts and piping allow for accessible maintenance and future changes while expressing their "engineering" functions.

The building is supported by a combination structure of precast concrete in the first two floors and a laminated wood frame of fir and hemlock beams bolted to fir columns in the remaining floors. Brush stucco fills the spaces in between columns. The engineering center consolidated several disparate offices and departments, including the dean of engineering along with the faculty of civil and industrial engineering, operations research, and the design division of mechanical engineering.

51. Herrin Hall and Laboratories   *Milton Pflueger, 1967*

Designed to consolidate the biological sciences in a compact complex of buildings, Herrin Hall and Labs replaced existing facilities in Jordan Hall in the northwest section of the Outer Quad. Built shortly after the completion of Pflueger's Graduate School of Business on the opposite side of the Oval, the biological sciences complex is a pair of four-story concrete pavilions with cantilevered balconies. Set at right angles to each other and joined by pedestrian bridges, the buildings enclose a three-sided grass court together

Terman Engineering

Herrin Hall and Laboratories

with the Gilbert Biological Sciences Building (1991), which opens onto Serra Mall. The buff-colored walls, the red-tile roofs, and the scale are remote echoes of the nearby Main Quad. The buildings are connected by covered walkways and pedestrian bridges, which expose the reinforced concrete frame along the outer edges. The bulk of the buildings, therefore, are recessed and cast in shadows from the passageways and the overhanging roof, which is somewhat reminiscent of the arcades fronting the quad.

52. John Stauffer Chemistry Buildings I to III

Clark, Stromquist, and Ehrlich, 1959–1966; Thomas Church, landscape architect, 1960–1966; conference gazebo, 1963–1965; Erlich–Rominger, renovation, 1995

The Stauffer lab buildings had been planned as early as 1954 as the centerpiece of a new chemistry quad designed by Spencer. The buildings, however, were built later by different architects. The Stauffer buildings contained facilities for organic chemistry, physical chemistry, and chemical engineering respectively. The work of Carl Djerassi, Henry Taube, and William Johnson, among others, has occurred and continues in these buildings. They are two-story concrete structures with aluminum sun louvers protecting the glazed labs. The concrete buildings were inspired by Spencer's earlier science

Stauffer Chemistry Buildings

buildings to the south and are linked along one end by a covered walkway, very much in the spirit of Mumford's recommendations to the planning office and Spencer's attempts to unify modernist buildings with an effective interpretation of the original quad. Birge Clark, a member of the art and architecture department, established the prototype for the Stauffer labs, whose internal organization is based on a modular scheme. Two polygonal-shaped classroom pavilions are located between the buildings.

53. Organic Chemistry Building *Spencer and Ambrose, 1948–1950*

Spencer designed a low-rise, inexpensive concrete block structure typical of his buildings for the science quad. To meet the changing needs of the scientists, he located the utilities in the outside walls, allowing the interior spaces to be reconfigured at will. Such solutions allowed Spencer to marry the practical and economic with his own modernist philosophy of design. The interior was divided into eight four-person labs, a specialized larger lab, a conference room, and a library area.

54. Seeley G. Mudd Chemistry Building

Clark, Stromquist, and Sandstrom, 1975–1977

Seeley G. Mudd Chemistry Building

Clark's brutalist interpretation of the reinforced concrete structure presents a variety of textured surfaces as its predominant aesthetic theme. The building's elevations are set under a long, overhanging red-tile roof, reminiscent of Spencer's own interpretation of the Main Quad's architecture. A little-used balcony surrounds the building at its second-floor level and is reached by stairs at either end, as in the Outer Quad's arcade. The balcony now connects to the Lokey Building.

55. Jordan Quad

Claude Oakland for Eichler Homes, architect, 1961–1964; Royston, Hanamoto, and Mayes, landscape architects, 1961–1964

Jordan Quad was built to relieve overcrowded conditions in several university departments and to house a new computation and data processing center. Oakland created typical Eichler architecture with a singular community of low-rise, post-and-beam, gable-roof buildings warmed by radiant heat. These are all features of Joseph Eichler's local housing subdivisions. The linear buildings are organized around garden courts and patios, and were intended to be connected by covered walks. Typical California vernacular features include fully glazed gabled entries within overscaled openings.

Jordan Quad

56. Center for Advanced Study in the Behavioral Sciences

Wurster, Bernardi, and Emmons, architects, 1954;
Thomas Church, landscape architect, 1954

Center for Advanced Study in the Behavioral Sciences

This center is an exemplary instance of Bay Area wood vernacular architecture and landscape planning by two of its most talented proponents. On the site of the demolished Charles Lathrop estate (some of the original barns and the gatehouse still stand), Wurster designed a clustered core of tall, single-story, dark-stained redwood buildings entered from breezeways and ringed by several low outbuildings. Each capitalizes on the commanding views of the San Francisco Bay to the east. William Wurster has managed a seamless mixture of public and private spaces, reflecting the importance of social interaction and the free exchange of ideas fundamental to the center.

The main pavilion is a low, wood-frame building with large expanses of glass and sliding glass doors enclosing a library, a cafeteria, and offices around several courtyards. The meeting room, an airy space of light redwood, has a laminated beam ceiling with cross-braces, while an adjacent study room has a white-painted brick fireplace set in back of the redwood paneling. The fully windowed walls make the spectacular landscape an integral ingredient of the interior spaces.

Linked by covered passageways and set down on the hillside, the private study wings offer blank facades toward the inner courts and gardens but glazed balconies to views and light. The site was selected as a retreat that would foster uninterrupted study, and Wurster accentuated this intention by bringing the major spaces into intimate contact with Church's landscape. Among its many accolades, the center won the American Institute of Architects Honor Award in 1958.

57. National Bureau for Economic Research

Wurster, Bernardi, and Emmons, 1974

Sited on a steep slope just below the firm's award-winning behavioral sciences building, the economic research building is a more modest stucco structure with classic Wurster touches. These included a glazed, two-story entry featuring a staircase rising against an abstract pattern of studs and mullions in a spectacular window wall. A chain-link cantilevered balcony rings the second floor. Its central corridor (now disfigured by duct work) is lighted by a high clerestory formed along offset angled roofs, a detail that is carried into the asymmetrically glazed side entry, giving this relatively simple building both visual tension and interest as well as dispelling the sense of a boxlike enclosure.

58. Radio Telescope *Stanford Research Institute, 1960–1962*

One of the Stanford's iconic images, the 150-foot aluminum-and-steel-trussed dish antenna, stands prominently in the foothills. It was the largest movable radio telescope in the country when built. Noted architectural critic Allan Temko wrote admiringly of the telescope and the linear accelerator as feats of modern engineering symbolizing a new technological age.

59. Stanford Linear Accelerator (SLAC)
Aetron–Blume–Atkinson and Charles Luckman Associates, 1961–1966

The two-mile long structure cuts relatively unobtrusively through the foothills and under Interstate 280 on its 480-acre site. The structure's interior is a striking piece of engineering, though this cannot be seen outside the building.

60. Stanford University Medical Center
Edward Durell Stone, architect; Thomas Church, landscape architect, 1955–1959; CRS, additions, 1976; NBBJ, renovation and modernization, 1987

The center was created out of the spirit of President Sterling's efforts to organize students, clinicians, and researchers into an effective "community of scholars." It combined the programs of the Palo Alto Hospital (Hoover Pavilion) with Stanford's old medical facilities in San Francisco, serving both the university's research and teaching objectives and the broader community's needs for an expanded hospital. The siting of the complex (three hospitals and four medical school buildings) on 56 acres near the burgeoning chemistry, biological sciences, and engineering quads was essential to Sterling's goals.

Architectural Forum praised the hospital as the largest in "modern times" and considered its "flattened-out" plan a radical innovation unlike the typical tower. Its formal **H** composition, which Stone felt echoed the university's main quad, consists of a center block containing the clinic and administrative facilities flanked by wings housing the Palo Alto Hospital and the medical school. The building's three stories, constructed of reinforced concrete with surrounding colonnades, were designed to accommodate related medical facilities on a single floor, while the flexible interior spaces abetted the constantly changing demands of clinical care, medical education, and research. Freestanding sun screens made of perforated, precast concrete grills cover the complex. A Stone trademark, these serve to harmonize the various pavilions and permit light to filter into the interiors of the buildings. Outdoor corridors, shielded by extensive roof overhangs and a colonnade, which Stone likened to the arcades and surface texture of the Main Quad buildings, were originally punctuated with sliding glass walls that could be opened to cooling breezes, hinting at the influence of Japanese shoji screens Stone said inspired this idea. A natural air-conditioning system was worked out using such vented corridors, along with fountains acting as cooling towers. The mass and texture of the block walls, Stone suggested, were also inspired by the original quads, as were the buff-painted finish and trim colors of terra-cotta red and brown.

The center was christened "the Garden Hospital" because of its extensive outdoor courts. Stone eased communication among the various pavilions of the complex by organizing them around a central landscaped court, other internal courtyards, outdoor roof terraces, and connecting covered arcades. Further alluding to the gardenlike aspects of the design, large hanging planters ring the building, helping to mitigate the uncompromising expanses of concrete. While establishing a more intimate scale, Stone further related his design to the original Olmsted campus plan by creating an approach inspired by Palm Drive and its Oval, with an open park and large fountain court in front of the main entry. This formal public avenue contrasted with the informal, off-axis relationship to the main campus.

Stone's complex aroused controversy at the time, prompting Herbert Hoover to urge the board of trustees to adopt Spanish style buildings that Hoover felt were both appropriate to California and memorialized "the spirit of learning and religious faith." Stone contended that his buildings were sympathetic to the Stanford vernacular, having almost the same scale, texture, and dimensions of the Outer Quad but were realized in more practical, modern day materials.

61. Hoover Pavilion *Reed & Corlett, 1931*

The Hoover Pavilion is Stanford's only example of a public works Art Deco building. A ten-acre site on the Stanford campus was leased by the city of Palo Alto, and the hospital was built to replace outdated facilities. A five-story, L-shaped structure built of pastel-painted reinforced concrete is

Hoover Pavilion

capped by a red metal roof on a central pyramidal tower set over the crossing of the wings. Art Deco terra-cotta details relieve the austere elevations.
An abstract, geometric fountain, echoing the spare, rectilinear detailing of
the pavilion's buttress-like walls, identifies the main entry along the north elevation. Beyond this elegant moderne portal, a vestibule staircase leads into
a large lobby that retains its original decorative meal grilles.

     The hospital was sited to serve both the city of Palo Alto and the
Stanford community and replaced the old Palo Alto hospital. In addition to its
eighty-beds, the hospital included wards for maternity, children, and students.
At the time it had such advanced features as sound-absorbing insulation in
the ceilings, air-conditioning systems, a refrigeration plant, and elevators. The
hospital was later incorporated in the Stanford Medical Center. It is currently
used for outpatient clinics and administrative offices.

62. Stanford Shopping Center

> *Welton Beckett, architect; Laurence Halprin, landscape architect, 1954–1957; Bull,*
> *Field, Volkmann, Stockwell, alterations, 1976*

Plans for a shopping center first appeared in the Skidmore, Owings, and
Merrill master plan of 1953. The now-defunct Emporium was the cornerstone of the $15 million regional shopping center. Built at a time when such
concentrated shopping centers were still a fresh experience, the Stanford
complex of stores is characterized by an open-air promenade that links the
various small shops along a corridor anchored at each end by two major

Stanford Shopping Center

retail stores. Fortunately Stanford never converted the open-air atmosphere into an enclosed, multistory mall. Stores have gradually been added to the 70-acre mall and designed by other architects, the most notable being Macy's (John S. Bolles, 1960).

Stanford Research Park

The Stanford Industrial Park was born in 1951 as a light manufacturing district. However, its focus on high-technology industry and research emerged in 1953. The 35-acre industrial park opened with the construction of the Varian Lab in 1953 and grew rapidly. By 1962 it had reached 360 acres accommodating forty-two lessees. By the early 1990s it had become a research park with some one hundred fifty companies occupying over 700 acres.

Organized along either side of a hilly corridor, Page Mill Road, and bordered to the south by Arastradero Road, the park has tried to retain its unobtrusive character amid mixed residential and commercial zones. One of its most accomplished creations was its landscape and zoning codes, which preserved a suburban residential, rather than industrial, feel, alas less evident in more recent large-scale additions. Spencer, as chair of a subcommittee on light industrial and commercial development for the university, devised a master plan for the park, which promoted a "social community" by excluding noticeably polluting industries. The subcommittee further urged that the architecture and landscaping support such a community by excluding "exaggerated site plans, structural forms or buildings which would impose themselves on the community." Buildings were limited to a height of fifty feet, with site plans that allowed for extensive open space and ample surface parking, with signage restricted to modest proportions.

The early park and its buildings exuded an inventive, even pioneering spirit, and freedom from convention whose goal was to enhance research through design. Although today these buildings may seem pedestrian, their architecture and landscaping reflected a functional ultra-modern styling, as in Hewlett-Packard's saw-tooth roof and its polychromed wall surfaces or in the unpretentious yet elegant General Electric building. Most of these earlier structures have been replaced. Several notable examples of this idea follow.

63. Hewlett-Packard Corporation Headquarters, 1501 Page Mill

Clark, Stromquist, and Sandstrom, architects, 1957–1958; Thomas Church, landscape architect, 1957–1958, 1965; Royston, Hanamoto, Mayes, and Beck, addition, 1965; Ehrlich, Heft, and Rominger, addition, 1969

Hewlett-Packard initially developed electronic testing and measuring equipment. The 140,000 square foot building was the most sophisticated structure the company had built to date. This structure still exudes the company's youthful confidence and ambitions. Originally located on an eight-acre site, the Hewlett-Packard headquarters epitomizes the space age thinking that often went into the design of buildings in the industrial park. These original buildings are boldly presented industrial sheds not usually associated with a company's headquarters, and sport fully glazed north walls, polychrome brick surfaces, and sawtooth factory lights (especially dramatic in the predawn hours or twilight). They exude the optimism of the opening of the electronics age. Inside, climate and acoustic controls regulated a critical environment for laboratory and factory facilities, as well as the administrative areas of the company. In a step beyond air conditioning, air was filtered electrostatically, and rooms were sound engineered.

Wall Street Journal

64. Wall Street Journal, 1701 Page Mill

Clark, Stromquist, Potter, and Ehrlich, architects; Royston, Hanamoto, Mayes, and Back, landscape architects, 1963–1965

This is one of the few early buildings and landscapes in the Research Park still largely unchanged. From Page Mill, the building extends over its site at an oblique angle to the street, rising quietly behind a sculpted grassy mound planted with trees. The building is essentially a low glass box sur-rounded by an arcade of concrete posts and shallow arches, echoing the Stanford quad. It is one of the few buildings in the park to attempt to do so.

65. Varian Associates Research and Development Laboratory, 611 Hansen Way

Original building *Erich Mendelsohn, 1953*
Later buildings *Rockwise and Watson*
Landscape *Thomas Church*

Varian was the largest producer of klystron tubes, which powered early radar defense systems and linear accelerators. German expressionist architect Erich Mendelsohn designed Varian's first building. Like the Hewlett-Packard building, this building, located off El Camino Real east of Page Mill Road, is set at angles to the street. Its long, single-story L-shaped plan rambles over the site like a large ranch house, an effect reinforced by the building's prominent gables and screening colonnade, though its clean lines and simple forms are reminiscent of the modern wood aesthetic of the San Francisco Bay Region.

66. General Electric (demolished)

John Carl Warnecke, architect; Thomas Church, landscape architect, 1954

General Electric

Now demolished, Warnecke's building on College Avenue was a paradigm of the unpretentious structural clarity and abstract beauty of the Park's ultramodern structures. The simple structural system became an aesthetic device while also allowing flexibility in handling the company's complex high-tech program. The handsome, long, single-story steel-frame and concrete structure was built in three stages forming an L-shaped plan. A tilt-slab construction system (popularized by Irving Gill in Southern California during the 1910s), where the concrete wall sections are poured on the ground and raised into place, afforded a simple, yet inexpensive construction method, which also allowed for the easy reuse of the walls in subsequent alterations. Further easing future changes, a concise eighteen-foot module was determined by the steel frame, and was filled by modular metal sash windows. Interior walls were of birch or fir plywood on studs, and the ceiling was exposed concrete slab.

Located at one end of the building's street front, the brick paved entrance was set into the two end bays of the open steel frame and marked by a pylon wall with the General Electric logo, suggesting the building's and the company's future growth. Trees were planted in the open-end bay, playfully marrying architecture and nature. Like most of Stanford Research Park buildings, parking was concealed behind the building. General Electric's laboratory developed microwave electron tubes that revolutionized the broadcast, communications, and radar industries.

*Aerial view of Meyer Library,
Law School, and CERAS*

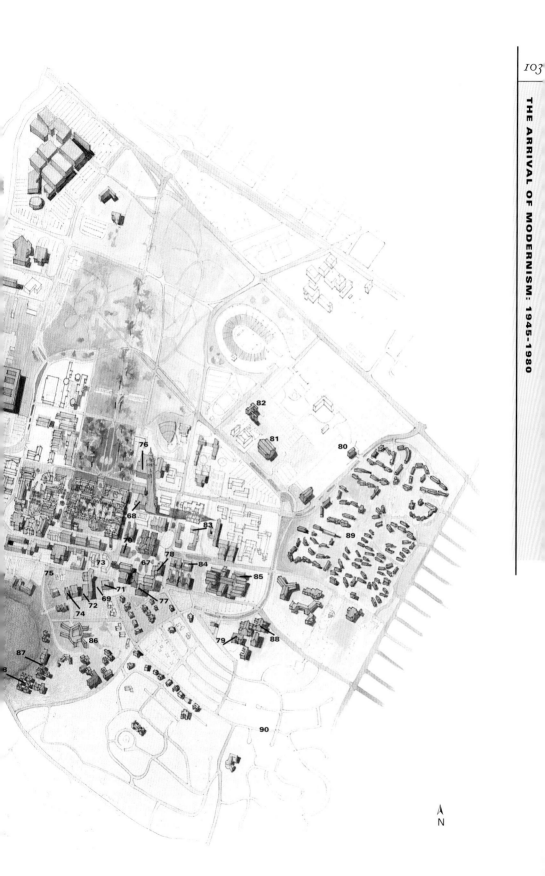

76

82

81

80

68

83

70

89

73

78

67

84

85

75

71

77

69

72

74

86

79

88

87

8

90

N

The Arrival of Modernism at Stanford

Prior to World War II, Stanford's steel and concrete structures had been disguised as distinct masonry-based styles, such as Toyon Hall or Hoover Tower. Afterwards, Stanford's building boom spawned concrete buildings, which were structurally expressive, inflated in scale, heavy in massing, and formal in composition. Characteristic features were attenuated piers, surrounding cantilevered balconies, lofty arcades, and red-tile roofs. Architects John Carl Warnecke, Eldridge Spencer, Milton Pflueger, and Skidmore, Owings, and Merrill left the most distinctive presence in concrete. Coupled with this new aesthetic makeup of campus architecture were Mumford's and Spencer's planning initiatives favoring independently sited buildings, rather than buildings organized around quadrangles.

As mentioned previously, Spencer advocated modern buildings that eschewed Stanford's conventional red-tile roofs, arcades, and buff-colored walls. Spencer's design for Stern Hall, a student dorm, aroused a storm of controversy chiefly among alumni who balked at its uncompromising flat roofs, blank and reinforced concrete walls and hard-edged angularity. Although Spencer mitigated the building's brash presence by organizing its low, horizontal blocks around courtyards reminiscent of the quad (the one concession to Stanford's architectural heritage), its lack of familiar and reassuring elements, especially red-tile roofs and arcades, provoked comparisons to bland industrial buildings. Spencer only inflamed opinion by stating that such elements as the arch and red-tile roof were meaningless in the 1950s. John Carl Warnecke countered Spencer's uncompromising modernism with traditional references that did not substantially diminish the contemporary appearance of his buildings, even if they introduced a note of conflict and ambiguity. Nevertheless, Warnecke's reputation rested on a sympathetic contextualism, years before the writings of Robert Venturi, growing out of the Bay Area traditions promoted by such architects as William Wurster. Within the Stanford vernacular, Warnecke's buildings were not always among his strongest designs

After 1960 Warnecke played a prominent role in Stanford's campus architecture and planning. Along with Gardner Dailey, Milton Pflueger, and Ernest Kump, as well as Thomas Church and Robert Royston, he was a member of Stanford's Architects Advisory Council, influencing the overall direction and character of the university's architecture and planning.

67. J. Henry Meyer Memorial Library

John Carl Warnecke and Associates; Thomas Church, landscape architect, 1960–1966

Meyer Library arose out of concerns that Stanford undergraduates were not "avid readers," and that a compelling environment was needed to entice students to browse and to read across disciplines. Meyer stands at the center of what was to be a new "Library Compound" ringed by low-rise academic structures (the surrounding screen was never built, making the library more dominant than intended). The site was a transitional zone between the academic and residential areas of the campus. Warnecke acknowledged this meeting of circulation routes by raising the building off the ground and creating a glazed entry lobby (now obscured) as a meeting area for students before ascending into the library's stacks.

The library was also to play an important campus aesthetic role by allowing access to and views of the building in all directions. It stood at one end of a larger complex of library buildings, including the education building, the old main library, and Hoover Tower and its proposed addition, all of which were to be linked by arcades and service tunnels. Meyer Library attempts to relate to these buildings in its heavy scale and massing, though it is mitigated in part by its skeletal structural articulation.

Roof terraces were provided, though easy accessways to outdoor courts and gardens were only partially completed. The building's piers and red-tile roofs are based on architectural elements taken from the Richardsonian Romanesque quads, though their tall and slender proportions, pierced

Rendering of Meyer Library

screen walls, and shallow precast concrete vaults give the building a light-ness and ascent more expressive of its own material construction; it is reminiscent of the earlier Stanford University Medical Center by Edward Durell Stone. The interior floor levels pivot around a central light well, creating an atrium-type space favored by Warnecke to bring light into the heart of a building. The main entry to the south, with its long, ceremonial staircase, was intended at one point to be flanked by two small buildings that were never built. Meyer now houses technological services and facilities for faculty and students and the East Asia Library.

68. Nathan Cummings Art Building

John Carl Warnecke and Associates; Thomas Church, landscape architect, 1969

Cummings Art Building

Proposals to build an art building had been advanced since the mid-1940s. In 1944 Lewis Mumford, then professor of humanities at Stanford, was asked to draw up a revitalized arts program concentrated within a single building on the site currently occupied by the art building adjacent to the art gallery. Mumford recommended not only studios, but also space to house and exhibit the museum's permanent collections. (The existing museum at the time was closed and considered too distant from the art department to be of use.) Lack of funds undermined its realization.

Under Lorenz Eitner, a new program was developed in the 1960s that lead to the construction of the current building. The reinforced-concrete building is planned around a sunken sculpture court that leads to a basement area with an auditorium, classrooms, and a slide library. The two stories above ground are in harmony with the scale of the adjacent art gallery. The main lobby serves an exhibition area lined with gray concrete walls and a waffled-concrete ceiling reminiscent of Louis Kahn's Yale Museum for British Art. To either side are administrative offices and the art library and the art studios. An upper outdoor balcony opens onto other studios housed along the rear.

69. Student Activities Center

Thomas Church, landscape architect, 1948–1960

With the sudden death of President Tresidder in 1948, the university sought to create a fitting memorial to pay tribute to his popularity among students. A few months after his death, a proposed Student Activities Center was announced, anchored by a student union named after the late president and sited immediately south of the old Union. Plans were developed, which included closing Lasuen and Santa Teresa Streets. This marked the beginning of the creation of a peripheral ring road (Campus Drive) around the campus rather than through its densest pedestrian areas, a recommendation initially made by Mumford.

Finally, in 1955, a new fifteen-acre student activities center was unveiled. Organized around an informal pedestrian corridor extending from the old Union past the site of the current post office (then only proposed), the activities center afforded facilities for cultural events, student government, recreation, dining, and a residential hotel. In contrast to the formality of the quad, the buildings were loosely sited to relate to their uses and their proximity to the foothills. The first phase of the program was the creation of a new music center (Dinkelspiel Auditorium) oriented along the curve of Lasuen and facing one block of a projected two block new student union (the second pavilion, never built, was to bridge Santa Teresa Street and connect with the old Union). The new union building contained a ballroom, lounge, and eating facilities in a building that was to resemble the music center in size and massing. The plan called for the casual dispersal of individual buildings, landscaped by Church, with the sole exception of the Warnecke bookstore and post office. The buildings were unified in style, scale, and materials, and connected by an arcade (now partly demolished) derived from that enclosing the courtyard of the old student Union across the way.

The new center was also planned to eliminate the need for large dining halls among the university's new dorms, and to enhance their intended social organization around small groups of students sharing common facilities. Such program decisions were made to try to restore the lost intimacy of Stanford's university life acutely felt after World War II when enrollment quickly doubled. Stanford's physical environment was not only meant to meet academic needs, but more importantly to foster a social training "in which the student can live as a participant," according to Spencer.

70. Post Office and Bookstore *John Carl Warnecke, 1959–1960*

Post Office and Bookstore

The post office and the bookstore replaced obsolete structures. (The wood and stucco post office, built in 1900 in the Richardsonian Romanesque style by Charles Hodges, also served as his office, a step up from the first wood shack located near Memorial Auditorium. The old post office was demolished to make ways for Dinkelspiel Auditorium. The mission style bookstore designed by Arthur Clark in 1905 was remodeled and served as part of the Career Planning and Placement Center until 2001.

The post office and the bookstore formed one side of the new activities center. The buildings are distinctive of Warnecke's "Stanford style": the red-tile roof elements set over colonnades composed of concrete piers carrying precast concrete vaults. The colonnade along the front echoes that of the old Union across the way, and more distantly the Main Quad. Originally the exterior was meant to be clad in sandstone veneer, but economies forced a change to marble-chip aggregate that was sandblasted. A covered colonnade across the back of the bookstore originally linked it with the post office, though this was partly removed when the bookstore was expanded in the 1960s.

Inside the bookstore, ninety-foot concrete bents, the thrust of which is taken up by the exterior arcades, support a one-hundred-foot-long skylight opening onto a double-height space that is ringed by a second-floor balcony. The building has an almost Wrightian feel as one passes under the arcade into a space that rises up dramatically into the light.

71. Florence Hellman Dinkelspiel Memorial
Auditorium *Milton Pflueger, with Spencer and Ambrose, 1955–1957*

Dinkelspiel Auditorium, the first phase of the activity center, was heralded at the time of its conception as the "theater of tomorrow." The soaring front of the building consists of a salient wall of smoke and mulberry-colored glass ninety feet across, a free interpretation of Eero Saarinen's Auditorium at the Massachusetts Institute of Technology. This emphasizes the theater's transparency. According to the stage designer, Arch Lauterer, earlier stages had been "opaque," relying on boxlike stages framed by a proscenium arch, creating the impression of a picture. The transparent stage, here fifty-six feet wide, swells out into the audience, eliminating any sense of separation between the two areas, with scenery projected onto the back wall

Dinkelspiel Memorial Auditorium, 1987

and lighting used to enhance an actor's motion and relation to others on the stage.

The fly loft was eliminated, and sets were moved onto the stage on wagons from storage areas in the wings. The loft, rear, sides, and gallery areas are now used for lighting. The tapered shape of the building, narrowing toward the stage, enhances the acoustic properties of the room, which has masonry sidewalls and a wooden rear wall that was originally lined with alternately sound-absorbent and sound-resistant panels laid on fiberglass blankets. The theater, it was felt, could thus present more intimate performances without the need for electronic sound amplification.

72. Tresidder Memorial Union

Spencer, Lee, and Busse, 1962

Tresidder Memorial Union

Tresidder Union was the flagship of the new student activities center, supplementing the 1920s union as the center of student life on campus. Initially, Tresidder Union was to be two separate buildings: one a social pavilion, with a stage and facilities for dramatic productions, and one a recreation hall. A single, two-story structure was built, offering a variety of student recreational and administrative services, which have changed over the years; these originally included a bowling alley, billiards, and table tennis on the lower level, and offices, reading and music listening areas, a large lobby opening onto conference rooms, program lounges, and exhibition space on the second floor.

Stylistically reminiscent of Warnecke's bookstore across the way, the long, buff-colored reinforced concrete and glass structure is ringed by a cantilevered balcony and capped by a red-tile roof with exposed rafters and heavy, laminated wood beams. The extensive, floor-to-ceiling glazing along the ground-floor dining areas, provide unimpeded views to the surrounding patios partially sheltered by the cantilevered second-story balcony. This enhances the sense of indoor-outdoor living, an effect complemented by interior ceilings of precast concrete panels, which undulate as if to suggest a tent-like covering.

The relationship between the indoor-outdoor areas is further enhanced by the continuous laminated wood beams that run through the building. A broad, spiral staircase set in front of translucent glass walls is a stylish 1960s touch and an important circulation element at the juncture of what was to be two separate buildings.

73. White Memorial Plaza

Thomas Church, landscape architect; Aristides Demetrios, sculptor, 1964

White Plaza is distinctive of Church's more formal work beginning in the 1950s. The site was a congested nexus of telephone poles, streets, parking lots, and temporary buildings. Church's design transformed the area with trees, walkways, and a sunken fountain court, which marked a transition between the quad and the activities center, making the plaza one of the more popular student gathering places on campus. At the four corners of the sunken court are curvilinear seats, suggesting a quatrefoil motif and the mission style references throughout the campus. The focal point of the landscape is the water fountain in bronze over copper. With its eighty jets its was meant to represent, according to the sculptor, "growth and growing

White Plaza Memorial

things" and the "ebb and flow" of students through the plaza, which was dedicated to the memories of two Stanford alumni, John Barber White II and William Nicholas White.

74. Faculty Club

Edward Page, architect; Thomas Church, landscape architect, 1965

Located on the fringe of the student activity center, the Faculty Club is a two-story wood-framed building with outdoor patios ringed by suites of dining rooms and a main dining hall. It also has Stanford's only on-campus hotel rooms. Church received a design award for his landscape plan.

75. Bowman House (Stanford Humanities Center)

Clark and Beuttler, 1952; addition, 1955; Hervey, Park, Clark, addition, 1957;
Freebairn-Smith Associates, addition, 1979

Bowman House (Stanford Humanities Center)

This unpretentious residentially scaled structure seems somewhat out of place amid the bustle of activities along Santa Teresa Street. Its openness to the nearby Donald Kennedy Oak Grove creates a strong sense of Stanford *place.* Formerly the headquarters of the Stanford Alumni Association, Bowman began its current use when the Frances C. Arrillaga Alumni Center (#133) was opened.

76. Graduate School of Business   *Milton Pflueger, 1966*

Established in 1925 with funds secured by Herbert Hoover, the business school occupied numerous locations both on and off campus before a permanent home was built. The school was built to "advance professionalism in business," to prepare students for management roles and scholarly research, to provide continuing education for business executives, and to fill the shortage of qualified business teachers.

The great bulk of this three-story, reinforced-concrete structure with bronze-anodized aluminum and glass curtain wall was inspired by the north flank of the Outer Quad, which Pflueger felt was necessary to its siting immediately next to the Oval. (Pflueger later complemented this composition of quad references with his biological sciences building

Graduate School of Business

directly across the Oval.) The building's monumental presence is mitigated somewhat by its sloping site, which provides a partially sunken
pedestrian corridor serving classrooms, a subterranean cafeteria, the
Bishop Auditorium, and a ground-level courtyard adorned with François
Stahly's bronze, *The Flame Birds* (1961).

From the side of the Oval, a grand stairway leads into a central, open
courtyard, following a spatial progression similar to that of the quad, with
staircases leading to the library on one side and to administrative offices on
the other. While the overall symmetry and massing around an open center
are reminiscent of the Outer Quad, the Pflueger building is organized around
a recessed central block with an open internal court and flanking blocks with
roof terraces and a surrounding cantilevered balcony, a feature distinctive to
many of Stanford's brutalist buildings. From the vantage point of the main
court, with its staircases and pedestrian corridors above and to the sides, and
flanking offices and library, the building highlights brutalism's fascination
with active urban elements in architectural design.

The reinforced concrete piers supporting the overhanging precast
concrete panels recall Warnecke's earlier bookstore and post office and contemporaneous Meyer Library. Warnecke commented that when the university rehired an architect, it allowed for stronger architectural uniformity
within the Stanford vernacular, with the various architects playing off each
other's work as well as their own.

77. Law School, Crown Quadrangle, and Kresge Auditorium

Skidmore, Owings, and Merrill, architect; Thomas Church, landscape architect, 1975

The law school, organized in 1908, had been housed in the Main Quad (Buildings 160 and 170). In 1945 Spencer proposed a modern design for a new law school building on the site currently occupied by Meyer Library, but the project was abandoned for lack of funds. In December 1965, with a renewed campaign of fundraising, planning for the law school began on a site that was to form part of an extended library quad.

Skidmore, Owings, and Merrill (SOM) designed four major buildings linked by arcades around the paved Canfield sculpture court, which opens to the north onto a grassy lawn landscaped by Church. Four-story Robert Crown Library is the largest of the buildings, though the James Irvine Gallery serves as the law school's "main street," feeding an enclosed courtyard, student meeting rooms, lounge, and conference rooms, and to the south, Kresge Auditorium. The buildings distantly interpret the Stanford vernacular using a refined version of the brutalist concrete approach with surfaces thinly ribbed and bush-hammered to create a corduroy texture, an expensive stylistic treatment even for its time.

The interiors use large graphics for important walls and bold colors throughout in an effort to "deinstitutionalize" the buildings. Such elements were felt to add a warmth and vitality to humanly scaled spaces accented by a variety of contemporary artworks. The lobby of the Crown Library is interesting for its red-hued interior, coffered ceiling, and central staircase with its large circular window lighting a basement stairway. Richman Hall has a dramatic skylit stairwell, and spaces for informal after-class meetings between faculty and students. The furnishings were chosen to enhance a casual living environment.

78. Center for Educational Research at Stanford

(CERAS) *Skidmore, Owings, and Merrill, 1971–1972*

SOM was already involved in the design of the new law quad when the university asked it to design what was initially called the Stanford Center for Research and Development in Teaching. CERAS, as it is now called, was to form one edge of a new quad, including the post office and bookstore, the new law school, Meyer Library, and at least one additional building. (Not only was this not realized but the plan demonstrated the extent to which the formal order of a quad had dissolved since Olmsted's day.) CERAS' odd rhombic form, however, allowed the architects to present substantial fronts toward the east and the south, where the building is a visual terminus of Alvarado Row.

The long side elevation of CERAS facing the lawn is a staggered series of terraces. The informal composition and warm red coloring reflect a time when the neutral tones and pure geometric plans of the reigning international style, which SOM had helped popularize since the 1950s, were increasingly coming under attack as sterile inventions. The building's skewed, glazed entry wall is carried through the center of the building forming an open, skylit court ringed by several floors of balconies, creating the impression of a lively town square.

The program's director, Robert Bush, adopted business approaches to open office planning to create a research and development environment that enhanced interaction. According to press accounts at the time, the center was the first academic institution in the country to employ an "open office landscape" that could be reconfigured as programs changed through the use of moveable partitions rather than solid walls. Flexible furnishings, supplied by Westinghouse's ASD design group, further aided shifting programmatic needs.

CERAS redefined the role of the educator promoting more humanized teaching through the development of the most advanced technology in teaching aids, including early computerized information retrieval and test systems.

79. Cowell Student Health Center *Ernest J. Kump Associates, 1966; demolished, 2002*

Cowell was sited near the campus's densest student housing area, directly adjacent to Kump's Cowell Housing Cluster, which mimics it in style. The two-story, board-form, concrete-textured building is domesticated with a surrounding wood pergola. The center, which for the first time consolidated student health services in one building, originally contained out-patient services and a forty-bed infirmary, was used only for clinics, counseling, and offices until replaced by the Allene G. Vaden Health Center (#137).

80. Stanford Federal Credit Union (formally School Construction Systems Development, Pilot Unit) *Ezra Ehrenkrantz, 1961–1964*

The Credit Union was an American prototype for "kit-of-parts" building systems that were developed during the 1950s and 1960s in England. Originally adopted for the mass production of low-cost schools, American versions allowed for greater variations by leaving the design of the external walls to

CERAS Building, looking through an arch of the Law School

Stanford Federal Credit Union

the individual architect hired by each school district. The Credit Union is distinguished from its European counterparts by its sleek dark metal and glass walls and cruciform posts, reminiscent of the work of Mies van der Rohe. The flexibility and economy of the system is evident inside, where roof trusses eliminate the need for interior columns. Mechanical systems are tucked into the roof space.

81. Roscoe Maples Pavilion *John C. Warnecke, 1969*

Maples Pavilion

Throughout the 1960s Stanford's athletics program gained increasing national recognition, prompting the creation of a master plan in 1967 and the construction of several significant buildings. The plan shifted the center of the athletics quad across Campus Drive away from the old Encina Gym to Maples Pavilion. Maples was based on a design Warnecke had prepared in 1957 for a radical new Stanford Sports Pavilion covered by a red-metal butterfly roof. Maples tripled the number of available seats to 8,000. Its steel space frame anchored at the corners provided unobstructed views from any seat. Maples was also conceived as a model space for concerts and other cultural activities in addition to sports events. The exterior highlights the stepped seating within, offering shelter below its reinforced concrete cantilevers. Corten steel, turning to a rust patina, clads the upper walls and is an abstract homage to the red-tile roofs of the quad buildings. Maples won the American Institute of Steel Construction's Award of Excellence in 1969 for aesthetic design in structural steel.

82. Dorothy and Sydney deGuerre Pools and Courts
Hawley and Peterson, 1973

The deGuerre pools and courts constituted phase II of the 1967 master plan, adding much-needed handball and squash courts, as well as an Olympic style swimming pool and water polo stadium next to Maples Pavilion. The area was further developed in 1999 (see #121 Avery Aquatic Center).

The dramatic rise in Stanford's student population following World War II, as well as its own depreciated housing facilities, prompted the construction of a series of new residence halls. The immediate influx of students was temporarily housed in the Stanford Village, the old U. S. Government's Dibble General Hospital in Menlo Park (now the campus of SRI International), which the university leased for a period of ten years during the construction of new dorms. For the most part, Stanford bucked the trend in postwar student housing toward the ever-popular high-rise building, exploiting instead its land holdings to implement a system of housing that was felt to foster academic and personal initiatives closer to its academic mission.

In this particular realm of campus architecture, Stanford experienced its most contentious debates about the continuity of its architectural traditions. Spencer's iconoclastic Stern Hall in particular brashly rejected the traditional ingredients, the red-tile roofs, arcades, and rough-textured, buff-colored walls, for the first time in campus history. Rather, its most obvious elements were drawn from the international style vocabulary of Walter Gropius, Mies van der Rohe, and Le Corbusier.

A few years later, William Wurster provided a regional approach to modernism with his Escondido Village apartments (phase I), an informally laid out community of cleanly detailed low-rise housing units of wood frame and stucco or concrete block. Its organization was reminiscent of Olmsted's original plan for the "cottage system" of picturesquely sited student housing for Stanford. Unlike the Beaux Arts formality of Bakewell and Brown's residences, Wurster's student housing clusters consist of a casually dispersed buildings in a parklike setting, reminiscent of Le Corbusier's urban proposal, though without its Cartesian geometry.

83. Crothers Hall   *Spencer and Ambrose, 1948; 1955*

Crothers Hall

This men's dorm for law students was sponsored by one of Stanford's early lawyers, George Crothers, an alumnus and friend of Jane Stanford. Crothers Hall anticipated the slightly later Stern Hall with uncompromising rectilinear accent and extensive glazing. Crothers had wanted a veneer of rough-cut stone, but Spencer's preference for smooth, planar, concrete surfaces prevailed. Unlike Stern Hall, Crothers had single rooms with a basement for social and study activities (added at Crothers' request), which was hailed as a significant innovation at the time. In the 1950s a second wing forming an open quadrangle was added to house engineering students.

Stern Hall

84. Stern Hall

Spencer and Ambrose, 1948; 1955, 1958, additions; Fisher–Friedman, architects, The SWA Group, landscape architects, renovation, 1995

The most controversial of Stanford's residences, Stern Hall was the first true international style building on campus. This men's dorm (it became coeducational in 1967) consisted of a complex of "houses" (only designated as such in 1954) partially inspired by a similar house system at Harvard and Yale. Stern was erected in stages, beginning with four houses in 1949 (Holladay, Fremont, Larkin, and Lassen), two more in 1956 (Donner and Serra), and the remainder in 1958 (Muir and Burbank). Each house was conceived as a microcommunity, complete with self-government and taxation.

A pamphlet for the dorm announced that residency was an important part of student life, serving as an "intellectual center" where a "significant part of learning and development takes place." These aspirations were fulfilled in part by the organization of the houses around internal courtyards with a central kitchen and dining facility serving the various houses. House libraries, lounge spaces, floor lounges, and faculty resident apartments were also included to facilitate greater interaction among students and faculty. Double-occupancy, two-room suites, consisting of a bedroom and a study, were thought to encourage greater academic excellence and social interaction.

Faculty, especially during the later 1950s, had urged changes in student housing standards to promote well-rounded pedagogic ideals. The earliest manifestation of this being in the later additions to Stern, its Muir and Burbank Houses. The university at the time declared its commitment to "an intellectual and friendly atmosphere conducive to high scholastic interest in cultural activities such as theater, art and literature and opportunity for members of the faculty to have closer, informal association with the students."

85. Wilbur Hall

Spencer and Ambrose, 1956; DES Architects, architects, The SWA Group, landscape architects, renovation, 1993

Wilbur Hall was built as a men's dorm (it became coeducational in 1967) to replace the aging Encina Hall. Capable of housing over seven hundred men, Wilbur was organized on a quadrangular plan with a kitchen/dining hall/administration unit at its center. Spencer had examined contemporary dorms of the day and discovered a preference for high-rise structures rather than the smaller residential units favored a decade earlier. Operating efficiency, social control, climatic conditions, and land values, according to Spencer, dictated the popularity of the high-rise option. However, Stanford's vast lands, and its preference for such architectural features as red-tile roofs and smaller living units with internal courtyards, promoted more sprawling housing complexes. Eight three-story housing blocks, designed to be perceived as distinct entities by the students, were symmetrically disposed around this center and were connected by covered walkways and exterior pedestrian bridges to it and lounges. The colors and materials of the buildings provided a homogenous element to the large complex and linked it to neighboring campus buildings.

Wilbur was considered an innovative experiment in designing "living groups" by including faculty residences. Between 1958 and 1959 Wilbur was converted into a house type dorm, creating small communities of students on each floor.

86. Florence Moore Hall

Milton Pflueger, 1956; The Steinberg Group, renovation, 1994

"Flo Mo," as Florence Moore is popularly known, was initially a women's dormitory and a further development of the house system the university implemented in its residences beginning in the late 1940s. Flo Mo replaced many of the older women's residences in service since the 1890s; in fact, several were torn down for the projected student activities center. Although Stanford abolished its limit of five hundred women students in 1933, the university insisted on housing all its women students, restricting their enrollment to two out of every seven applicants. The university also believed that women had "special needs" that affected the design of their dorms. In 1955 a Committee of the Association of Women Students was formed to detail their requirements. The committee's findings were turned over to Pflueger, and its impact was reflected in the design of Flo Mo's seven three-story living units organized loosely around an internal courtyard with central offices and service facilities.

Each wing contained fifty students and had its own social lounge and dining room with adjacent outdoor patio and sundecks. Each floor included a sitting room with a kitchenette and resident assistant's apartment. Stanford felt that the dining hall was a fundamental means of encouraging "social development and education in good citizenship" among residents and made it an integral part of its housing program. Each living unit, therefore, helped foster a sense of identity among the relatively small groups of students. In 1969 two houses were given over to men's dorms, making the dorm coeducational.

The Knoll (center) and Florence Moore Hall (background)

87. Undergraduate Men's Student Housing Cluster I and Undergraduate Student Housing Cluster II

Undergraduate Men's Student Housing Cluster I (Kappa Sigma, Theta Delta Chi, Sigma Alpha Epsilon, Phi Delta Theta, and Row Housing Office)
  John Carl Warnecke, architect; Laurence Halprin, landscape architect, 1960–1962
Cluster II (Enchanted Broccoli Forest, 353 Campus Drive, 664 Lomita Drive, 685 Lomita Court, Lambda Nu, and Faculty Residence)
  John Carl Warnecke, architect; Laurence Halprin, landscape architect, 1963–1965

Following a critical report on its fraternities in 1957, Stanford adopted a "house" policy requiring clustered units, each containing approximately fifty students, served from a common kitchen. Within each cluster was a resident faculty fellow. The plan was especially directed toward the nine hundred students housed in fraternities, gradually bringing them under the university's housing program for the first time, though the policy was also intended to create a stronger integration of the social and the academic spheres of life.

Warnecke's clusters were the first residences to reflect the new attitude. The houses were organized around social and study spaces, such as the residential library or the communal dining hall. The university wanted to build cohesive yet independent house units so as to instill a sense of self-government and identity within the student population. For example, students were allowed to choose their residences and to name their houses.

Long corridors typical of earlier residences were eliminated, facilitating greater internal circulation and more effective student interaction. Warnecke segregated these functions into distinct clusters of three to six units consisting of one- to three-story redwood and stucco buildings, each holding fifty students in modular bedroom style suites. The housing clusters casually climb the slope of the hill near Lake Lagunita, creating an irregular plan and silhouette.

The design employed big, simple shapes for the dorms and wrapped the social areas in colonnades. The units were painted in light colors ranging from white to beige, and were capped by hipped red-tile roofs. The seemingly random placement of balconies and windows further accentuates the informality of the whole. In 1964 the four first houses received an Award of Merit for Excellence from the Community Facilities Administration, a branch of the federal Housing and House Finance Agency.

88. Cowell Undergraduate Men's Housing Cluster III

(Whitman, Zeta Alpha Phi, Terra, Alpha Tau Omicron, and Alpha Sigma Phi)
Ernest J. Kump Associates, 1967–1969; Thomas Church, landscape architect, 1967–1969; Cody Anderson Wasney, renovation, 1998

Kump's loose confederation of buildings was organized around a large lawn. Each building has its own plan, though similar stucco, plywood, and concrete wall materials unified the structures. The elevations are marked by a series of round-headed windows and doors on the first floor with windows set under the deeply overhanging eaves. Their interiors were disposed around an interior stairwell leading to double-loaded corridors with studies and bedrooms. Large living rooms and dining rooms were located on the ground floor.

89. Escondido Village

Escondido Village I *Wurster, Bernardi, and Emmons; Thomas Church, landscape architect, 1959*
Escondido Village II, III, and IV
Campbell and Wong, 1964–1971; Royston, Hanamoto, and Mayes, landscape architects, 1964; Mayer and Beck, landscape architects, 1966
Escondido Village V *Ned H. Abrams; Anthony Guzzardo, landscape architect, 1971*

Escondido Village was built originally to house married students at a time when the scarcity of such accommodations was considered to be the most critical housing problem then facing American universities. It was also built to replace the aging Stanford Village. The new Village was designed in five stages on one hundred seventy-five acres with approximately fifteen hundred living units with a two-hundred foot buffer zone maintained between the housing complex and the city. The master plan is organized by a ring road that serves a series of geographically distinct communities, each of which is planned along this access route picturesquely lined with one- and two-story concrete block or woodframe buildings (the multi-story apartment towers were added beginning in 1964).

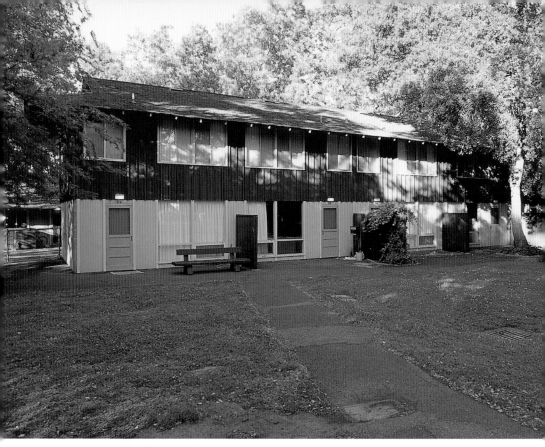

Escondido Village

Spencer, who served as supervising architect, noted that the goal of the village was to "create a stimulating, refreshing environment which will give incentive to cultural endeavor." Its success relied on avoiding regimentation and dispersing "the housing in a landscape of open fields and wooded areas rather than erecting rows of buildings with formalized planting...consciously avoiding an institutional feel." The sense of community was reinforced by the addition of the Bing Nursery School (Clark, Stromquist, Potter, and Ehrlich) in 1966 and a community center in Escondido Village V in 1971.

Wurster had been recommended both by Mumford and Warnecke at various times as a consultant on Stanford's planning. His EV I consisted of one- and two-story garden-type apartments adopted from the "long, low lines of early California ranch houses with low pitched shingle roof and wide eaves." The 250 living units are low-rise buildings overscaled by deep overhangs with grey cement board with redwood board-and-batten walls and siding with trim in soft, contrasting colors, and concrete block end walls. The closed fronts of the two-story buildings give way inside to double-height living areas with loft spaces and open along the back onto a patio linked by communal play areas. The apartments are radiant heated, and internal and party walls are soundproofed with fiberglass insulation. Wurster designed seven types of apartments, with one, two, and three bedrooms, varied by height, balconies, or loft spaces. The apartments are clustered in groups of two and three buildings with shared grass courtyards, landscaped with trees and fenced to provide secure play areas for children providing "thorough-fares" for wagons and bicycles. The later additions by Campbell and Wong are sympathetically integrated, with the high-rise buildings discretely sited.

Each community is identified by name—Blackwelder, Hoskins, and so forth—and linked by landscaped spaces that serve as larger social areas. Campbell and Wong's textured, reinforced concrete towers add a contrast-ing vertical dimension to Escondido's overall horizontal layout, evoking a picturesque adaptation of Le Corbusier's skyscrapers in the park. In fact, the towers, which offer unrestricted views from each apartment, were compared in press reports to those in Latin American countries where Le Corbusier's influence was strong. The tower contains lobbies and lounges for social events.

Although adjacent to Escondido Village, Mirrielees is an oddity with a strange four-story Y-shaped plan, the result of student recommendations and the economics of being built by Levitt and Sons of California. The angled plan was thought to permit more balconies offering better views and small private gardens for the ground floor apartments. In 1972 Abrams also added a multipurpose building, now the community center, and converted the old Escondite Cottage into the administrative building.

90. Frenchman's Road, Pine Hill Road, and Lathrop Drive—Faculty Houses

Following World War II the university planned several subdivisions to attract and "retain faculty as part of a social group." The university recog-nized faculty housing as an important avenue fostering interdisciplinary exchanges even prior to the construction of a significant faculty club (1960s). Housing tracts pushed Mayfield Avenue to its eastern edge along Stanford Avenue, one of the borders of College Terrace, and south into the Pine Hill region, where two subdivisions were built in the late 1950s and early 1960s, both landscaped by Geraldine Knight Scott. Southwest of the campus along Sand Hill Road was the Stanford Hills subdivision, started in 1957 and laid out by Skidmore, Owings, and Merrill, the only realization of its 1953 master plan. Unlike those in Pine Hill, these houses were mostly California ranch houses (encouraged by the university) and made available to the general public as well as to the Stanford faculty.

These latter subdivisions were professionally landscaped (the utilities in the Pine Hill subdivisions were buried) and exploited their hilly terrain and vistas; they often included small public parks, schools, and community spaces. The 116 lots available in Pine Hill I ranged in size from 11,000 square feet to 34,000 square feet over a forty-acre parcel. Scott perpetuated the "wooded atmosphere of the arboretum," staggering street plantings to avoid regimentation, and employed a variety of shapes, colors, and textures to "produce brilliant spring and fall coloring." Flowering shrubs and trees enhanced buffer zones, and trees that lose their leaves in the fall were planted along southern exposures, taking advantage of solar orientation. Pine Hill II was organized on steep slopes around a three-acre park planted with live oaks, maples, acacia, and other trees. The 120 homesites covering seventy-five acres and platted in lots ranging from 12,000 square feet to 26,000 square feet, were also protected by buffer zones and exploited spectacular views of the bay and the foothills.

Stanford Hills subdivision was sited on thirty acres of rolling hills dotted with native oaks as the first stage of a 940-acre, 1,876-homesite development meant to house some 20,000 people. SOM had developed the master plan over two and a half years. The sizes of the lots varied from a quarter acre to 5 acres and included communal spaces for parks, playgrounds, and schools, which were approached by foot and bike paths. The plan called for linking the various neighborhoods by collector roads, which served the smaller, low-traffic local streets.

These regions of the campus predominantly feature modern Bay Area architecture, including work by Eichler Homes, A. Quincy Jones and Frederick Emmons, Claude Oakland, Robert Anshen and William Stephen Allen, William Wurster, Aaron Green, and Roger Lee. There is also a fine representation of local architects, Victor Thompson, Morgan Stedman, and William Hempel in particular. Walking or driving along the streets of the subdivisions reveals a continuity in planning between the oldest and the latest developments in the informal landscaping of the streets and the continuity of the architectural styles. Examples include:

Morrell House, 715 Frenchman's Road *Jones and Emmons for Eichler Homes, 1961*

Margolis House, 724 Frenchman's Road *Jones and Emmons, 1965*

Dodds House, 729 Frenchman's Road *KEM Weber Designers, 1949*

Weissbluth House, 820 Pine Hill Road *Jones and Emmons, 1958*

Creighton House, 823 Pine Hill Road *Jones and Emmons, 1959*

Merryman House, 835 Pine Hill Road *Anshen and Allen, 1959*

Heffner House, 844 Pine Hill Road

> *Wurster, Bernardi, and Emmons, architect; Geraldine Knight Scott, landscape architect, 1958*

Leiderman House, 828 Lathrop Drive

> *Jones and Emmons, architects; Hanamoto, Meyes, Beck, landscape architects, 1963*

Chung House, 903 Lathrop Drive *Victor Thompson, 1962*

Huntley House, 796 Cedro Way

> *Wurster, Bernardi, and Emmons, architect; Geraldine Knight Scott, landscape architect, 1962*

Fletcher House, 773 Mayfield Avenue *Henrik Bull, 1965*

91. Oak Creek Apartments, 1600 Sand Hill Road

Warnecke and Associates, architect; Laurence Halprin, landscape architect, 1959; Wurster, Bernardi, and Emmons, 1968

In his 1947 planning report, Lewis Mumford recommended as one of several regions for residential development on Stanford lands, this area bordered by San Francisquito Creek and Sand Hill Road, the site of Leland Stanford's estate. Subsequently, the southern portion of this land was leased to a private developer to build an apartment complex. The first construction began with Warnecke's two-story wood buildings on a triangular piece of land at the extreme southern end of the Sand Hill property. Three interconnected structures with carports were organized around a central landscaped mall by Halprin, which featured a large circular bowl with meandering paths leading to it. The project received an AIA Award of Merit in 1967.

The majority of the buildings are in a second phase by Wurster, Bernardi, and Emmons. Siting their buildings along Sand Hill Road on a relatively narrow strip of land next to the creek, the firm dispersed the low-rise buildings on either side of an entrance court. The concrete and masonry buildings were varied in their plans and massing though unified in their earth-tone colors and repetitive elements, creating a lively community of modest apartment structures.

Nearing the Centennial: 1980–1991

109

102

Rains Housing and East Campus

105

106
103

96
97
93
2
95
107
101

99
100
94

110

108 →

N

Postmodernism and the Historical Context

As Stanford's centennial neared, President Donald Kennedy oversaw a record-breaking fund-raising campaign. Its cornerstone was to be the creation of a new $250 million science and engineering quad, touted as the "nation's largest effort to renovate and expand research facilities on a university campus." However, only two buildings were constructed before the devastating 1989 Loma Prieta earthquake.

The proposed science and engineering quad typified the post-modern style of much campus architecture during the 1980s. Emphasizing lightweight, decorative, and colorful interpretations of Stanford's vernacular red-tile roofs, arcades, and rough-faced sandstone walls, postmodernism was fundamentally at odds with the heavy and austere character of the Romanesque-Mission style of the Main Quad. More curious and disturbing, since postmodernism holds contextualism and historicism in high regard, was a pattern of development that at times threatened the remaining integrity of Olmsted's plan, as in the decision to site Littlefield Center partly within the wilderness area around the Oval. At its best, however, as in the Haas Center by William Turnbull Associates, postmodern principles provided good architecture and site planning, and a fine marriage between past and present traditions.

In the late 1980s the Board of Trustees identified several major capital needs that would prepare the university for the twenty-first century. Among these were housing for both faculty and students, the remodeling of outdated and seismically inadequate facilities, and the construction of new buildings that would serve the latest areas of academic research, such as artificial intelligence and superconductivity. An estimated 3.8 million square feet of additional floor space was proposed for the campus, ranging from the development of the Near West Campus, the School of Medicine, and the Stanford West region along Sand Hill Road.

92. Paul Allen Center for Integrated Systems

Ehrlich-Rominger, 1984

The first postmodern interpretation of Stanford's architectural vocabulary, the Allen Center, has beige-painted stucco walls, an off-center decorative steel-barrel-vaulted entry, and a metal colonnade set under a red metal shed roof. Along one side, an interlace pattern of decorative metal whimsically plays off Quad references. The entry centers on a view of Hoover Tower, though the building's siting is oddly out of alignment with its neighbors and the traditional Olmstedian axes. The 70,000-square-foot building epitomized the synthesis of research, teaching, and practical application of

theory first adopted by President Sterling's administration. The interior spaces were designed to promote interaction among faculty and students from distinct disciplines. The heart of the building is an integrated circuit lab that produced VLSI (Very Large Scale Integration) computer chips. Around it are general labs, conference rooms, computer rooms, and sixty-five offices for faculty and students.

Paul Allen Center for Integrated Systems

93. Littlefield Management Center

Kohn, Pedersen, Fox with McLellan and Copenhagen, 1988

Littlefield Management Center

Littlefield Center remains a controversial building: it violated Olmsted's wilderness near the Oval and straddled Lasuen Mall, one of the last significant Olmsted arteries. Standing within view of the Outer Quad, Littlefield lacks the heaviness and deeply textured walls of those buildings; Littlefield's surfaces appear thin and almost weightless. The colonnade along the ground floor follows the U-shaped plan, interrupted at the building's center by a small arched opening, before continuing along one arm as a free-standing, red-tile roof passageway that awkwardly bangs into the older business school. The colonnade in darker colored precast concrete adds mass along the base of the building. Short, squat towers rise through the corners of the three-story building; however, tall, narrow, double-story windows separated by an inset decorative wood panel and other surface ornamentation only enhance the lightness of the overall building. Currently Littlefield provides facilities for the Graduate School of Business, as well as large conference rooms for the university's board of trustees.

94. Braun Music Center *Marquis Associates, 1979–1984*

Braun exemplifies the campus's concern with connection. Sited at the edge between the activities center and the student residential area, Braun literally attempts to bridge the two regions, straddling Lasuen Mall, a pedestrian corridor. Its long, linear plan consciously lies askew of the Main Quad's east-west axis, which determines the orientation of most of the campus buildings. In this alignment, it tries to mitigate the Main Quad's axial formality and picturesque, curving Mayfield Avenue, thereby encompassing the formal and informal dimensions of Olmsted's planning at Stanford. The music center also forges links with the neighboring Dinkelspiel Auditorium and somewhat contains White Plaza by defining the activities center's southern boundary.

Braun's chief architectural feature is its semicircular glazed portal that marks the second-story bridge over Lasuen Mall and attempts to recall the long-lost Memorial Arch entry to the Main Quad or the quad's arcades. Opening onto an atrium-type space, the bridge connects the music center's two wings—its studio and recital hall to one side, the library and classrooms to the other. The light-buff building's perimeter corridors are glazed entirely along both stories with offset mullion patterns that are carried into the textured stucco wall surfaces. Along the ground floor are massive Doric-style columns with a necking ring of red tile, a postmodern reuse of a traditional decorative motif that is also picked up at the parapets of the flat roofs on the building's ends.

Braun Music Center

95. Science and Engineering Quad, Near West
Campus *The Architects' Collaborative, 1985–1987*

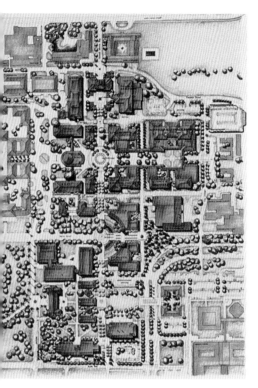

Near West Campus Plan

Sited in Olmsted's first plans, a west quad dedicated to science and engineering had been designed as early as the 1920s, and again during the building program of the 1950s, when it was partially realized. In the mid-1980s, university president Kennedy proposed an ambitious redevelopment strategy designed to give a quadlike character to this region of the campus, ending its history of independently sited buildings that continually pushed out the campus's western edge. The Near West Campus plan was also designed to reconnect this region with that of the quad by adopting a master plan that called for an orderly arrangement of buildings organized and unified by landscaping, major nodes, and axes, concentrating related academic departments within specific regions.

The plan proposed a new north-south mall linking the Terman Engineering Center through the Near West Campus area to the biology and chemistry area. A major focal node behind the now demolished Physics Lecture Hall defined a cross-axis. One of the most dominant design features was to be an exedra of two buildings, occurring at the closure of Serra Street just past its juncture with a new north-south mall. This termination of another of Olmsted's principal axes would have completed the abandonment of the original plan's axial order; however, this region plan did at least provide for controlled growth and did recommend harmony in architecture and landscape.

96. William M. Keck Science Building

McLellan & Copenhagen, 1985

Keck Science Building

This massive structure, cleft in the center by a three-story glazed atrium, marked the beginning of the development of the Near West Campus plan. Designed to house "surge" labs for the departments of biological science, chemistry, and chemical engineering, Keck was completed within a year. Its exterior walls, composed of polymer-coated styrofoam, are detailed like heavy ashlar masonry blocks, immediately recalling Peter Behrens' 1909 masterpiece, the AEG Turbine Factory in Berlin. Keck was sited as a northern anchor to the chemistry quad of the Near West Campus plan. An unfortunate consequence of this siting is that Keck looms over Stanford' major cultural region, the museum and its sculpture garden. Keck's most impressive features is its central lobby-atrium rising three stories to a tentlike skylight, though the banal, industrial-strength details are boldly overscaled and out of character with surrounding structures.

97. Charles H. Gilbert Biological Sciences Building

Arthur Erickson Associates with McClellan and Copenhagen, 1988–1991

Gilbert Biological Sciences Building

The Gilbert building embodies "adaptable design concepts, fast-tracked building techniques, and funding strategies" first developed with the Keck Science building. Designed to foster a cooperative working environment more stimulating to researchers than being housed in isolated departments, the building is organized to house groups of faculty sharing facilities on each floor. It completes with the Herrin buildings a three-sided grass court, which opens toward Serra Mall. Pedestrian bridges connect the Gilbert building with the Herrin Labs. The length of Gilbert's sand-colored precast concrete wall surfaces are broken up by bands of green glass that are alternately inset along flat planes angled into the walls or bowed out. At ground level toward Serra Mall, the Gilbert building sits well below grade, where a faceted, curving glass wall is recessed under a cantilevered building mass. Along the flanks, the labs and office step out over coupled columns, which then carry through the elevations as single shafts. The paired columns are a postmodern reminiscence of those of the Main Quad and lend the building an uneasy lightness along its base. An incongruous red-tile roof partially conceals a formally composed greenhouse and mechanical penthouse clad in prepatinated copper. The roof eaves are green-hued glass projecting over a similarly glazed attic story. The overall effect is rather disjointed in impression and expressive of an unsuccessful attempt to pull modernism, postmodernism, and Stanford's traditional architectural vocabulary into one design.

Cogeneration Facility

98. Cogeneration Facility *Spencer Associates, Kaiser Engineers, 1988*

This streamlined, prefabricated metal structure creates a striking presence along Campus Drive West. Its dull green metallic hue blends well with the heavy oak planting in the foregrounds. This facility provides the high temperature water, chilled water, and electricity for nearly all of the central campus and medical center.

99. Sweet Hall *Spencer Associates, 1986*

Sweet Hall, a postmodern structure, was designed to consolidate undergraduate services, including computer clusters (LOTS) and training and support programs (IRIS), Stanford Overseas Studies, and the Undergraduate Advising Center. Its siting attempts to complete the library quad envisioned much earlier by Warnecke.

100. Clock Tower *Esherick Homsey Dodge and Davis, 1983*

Clock Tower

Memorial Church originally included a large belfry, which in 1901 was fitted with duplicates of London's Winchester chimes. When the tower collapsed in the 1906 earthquake, the University preserved the chimes until it built a new freestanding structure immediately behind the church across Escondido Mall at the head of Duena Street. This tapered, shingle style tower with an open carillon survived until 1967, when it was torn down to open the street to Escondido Mall. The chimes were rehoused in this new Clock Tower with its attached, colonnaded pergola at the intersection of Escondido and Lasuen Malls.

101. Serra Complex *Yandell, Crosby Architects, 1988*

Serra Complex garden

These two L-shaped, tilt-up concrete buildings, with tile roofs over wood-detailed eaves, enclose a garden modeled on traditional French themes. The buildings are very similar in style to several built earlier in the research park and in other nearby office developments. They currently house administrative departments, including the University Architect/Planning Office.

102. Artists' Studio *Alton S. Lee and David A. Lee, 1987*

This well-designed wood-frame building, located in the foothills adjacent to the golf course, is designed as a retreat for faculty of Stanford's art department.

103. Falk Cardiovascular Research Building (CVRB)

Hellmuth, Obabta, Kassabaum, 1984

Falk Cardiovascular Research Building

This facility, developed to house the research of Dr. Norman Shumway, the pioneer of heart transplant surgery, was sited and planned for a direct connection to the hospital's surgery suite. This connection was never built because of building code restrictions; this building now stands isolated from other medical school buildings to the south.

104. Beckman Center for Molecular Biology

MBT Associates, 1988

Beckman Center

This pastel-hued modernist concrete building is the tallest academic struc-ture at Stanford. Its L-shaped form surrounds a well-landscaped entry courtyard with a multi-storied curved glass wall. Though praised for its func-tionality, its colors, articulation, and huge scale seem ill at ease with the adjacent E. D. Stone complex.

105. Arboretum Child Care Center

MacDonald Architects; Les Baronian, landscape architect, 1987–1988

Arboretum Child Care Center

The facility is composed of simple, nicely detailed, wood-frame, gable-roofed buildings organized around an internal courtyard.

106. Lucile Salter Packard Children's Hospital

Anshen and Allen, 1991

Lucile Salter Packard Children's Hospital

The award-winning design is an informal series of stepped, landscaped terraces around an interior landscaped courtyard. The hospital is connected to the Stanford University Hospital at a 90-degree angle, thus giving the children's hospital its own entrance from Welch Road. Its beige-coated styrofoam walls and tile accents give a postmodern recall of Stanford's traditional elements more than Stone's richly textured concrete medical center complex. Repetitive striations underscore the building's steel-framed construction. The central atrium with its landscaped garden brings light and greenery into the building, thus mitigating the sense of hospital confinement.

107. Ford Center for Sports and Recreation and Ford Quad

ELS/Elbasani and Logan, architects; The SWA Group, landscape architects, 1990

Ford Center and Quad

This postmodern building is sited to form a three-sided quad with two of Bakewell and Brown's athletic buildings. Use of beige limestone, buff stucco, and tile roof recall the central campus palette. The Ford Center's large, semicircular windows and heavy mullions echo those of the now demolished Encina Gymnasium; however, its minimal roof overhang is unique to Stanford. The Ford Center houses two large gymnasiums; one dedicated to gymnastics and the other used for intramural sports. A skylit spine attaches the center to the Burnham Pavilion, the university's first basketball court, also by Bakewell and Brown. This facility has been renovated for volleyball, wrestling, gymnastics, and recreation.

The university's phenomenal growth since World War II continued to drive Stanford's housing priorities during this period. With an ever increasing student population, expanding research park, and pioneering science and engineering departments attracting more faculty, the university had pushed the demand for housing beyond its ability to support the increasing demands. Expediencies for temporary student housing were approved, probably the most drastic of which was the creation in 1967 of a trailer park known as Manzanita Park (recently demolished).

Stanford's housing shortage reflected national trends. Yale, Cornell, Harvard, and other institutions simultaneously prepared studies in the late 1960s exploring alternatives. Stanford organized two committees within months of each other in 1969 and charged them with looking into "alternative approaches to major housing issues." President Pitzer's ad hoc housing committee urged the creation of 600 to 2,000 low-to-moderate cost housing units on 75 to 100 acres as soon as possible, "to encourage a broad spectrum of people of various interests, races, religions, occupations, and all ages to reside in Palo Alto in order to provide a fullness of social interrelationships." The committee identified possible building sites including the foothills near Junipero Serra Boulevard and Page Mill Road. Its proposals advanced policy for much subsequent housing on campus land, such as the Oak Creek and Stanford Hills subdivisions, which were designed both for the Stanford community and others not affiliated with the university.

However, beginning in the 1970s, neighborhoods in Palo Alto and Menlo Park repeatedly challenged university plans to build on what was perceived to be "open space," an issue that has plagued the current development known as Stanford West, a project that had been surrounded by controversy for more than ten years. Student housing on campus saw only two significant developments in the 1980s, the Rains Apartments and Governor's Corner, while only Peter Coutts and Ryan Court Housing were being built for faculty and staff.

108. Peter Coutts Housing

Fisher-Friedman Associates, architect; Anthony Gazzardo, landscape architect, 1979–1983

The proposal to locate housing on Frenchman's Hill was first studied in 1971 in response to the university's housing recommendations. Known as Frenchman's Terrace, the project consisted of 225 two-story townhouses clustered on twenty acres. Although 50 percent of the land remained as a landscaped park, concerns about dwindling regional open space prompted

Peter Coutts Housing

protests to the university's plans. In the end, the project, sponsored by the Mid-Peninsula Urban Coalition, failed when the federal government declared a moratorium on housing loans in 1973 and withdrew funding two years later.

In 1979 the project was revived and a new plan was formulated. Fisher-Friedman Associates was asked initially to prepare several proposals for 200 units combining townhouses and flats on the twenty-acre site on Frenchman's Hill. The project was scaled down to 140 units, offering a spectrum of housing sizes ranging from 1,200 to 1,500 square feet. The townhouses have informal, open plans with loft spaces, reached by spiral staircases, and outdoor decks. The complex is organized around a loop circulation road with green spaces and a central park area featuring a community building and swimming pool. The shingle style houses offer irregular silhouettes and constantly changing vistas along the different elevations with tall chimneys, steeply angled gabled and half-gabled roofs, and overscaled dormers set atop projecting bays above garages. Partly sheltered balconies and large picture windows provide a hint on the exterior of the open plans inside. Along the rear elevations the townhouses step up and down over the site and are provided with first-floor patios and second-story cantilevered balconies shielded by slatted sun louvers. The heavy landscaping sets the final tone for this well-designed, award-winning project.

109. Governor's Corner Student Housing

Esherick Homsey Dodge and Davis, architects; Nashita and Carter, landscape architects, 1983

Governor's Corner Student Housing

On the western fringes of the main campus is Governor's Corner, eleven student residences on 22 acres housing some 800 students around a large greensward and interspersed with multipurpose community areas. The rural setting offers a contrast to many of the campus's more formal quadlike spaces. Governor's Corner extends the precedents established by both Warnecke's and Kump's housing clusters, where the units were both detached

and personalized, in contrast to the uniformity of Spencer's Stern Hall. The
randomly dispersed three-story clusters are differentiated in plan and contain suites of no more than six single-occupancy rooms with their own lounge.
The simple cubic forms of the houses, the detailing, and the ochre and russet
stucco walls suggest the spare interpretations of the Mission style by Bakewell
and Brown in the next door Lagunita Court. Among the facilities are a program center, dining hall, eating clubs, and guestrooms. The residences are
named after former Stanford faculty and staff known for their contributions to
undergraduate education.

110. Liliore Green Rains Apartments

Backen, Arrigoni & Ross, architects; The SWA Group, landscape architect, 1988

Liliore Green Rains Apartments

This award-winning housing complex
provides rooms for almost 800 graduate students. The plan of the twelve-
acre site follows the gentle curve of
Bowdoin Street before turning sharply
north, where it intersects with Escondido
Road and the neighboring graduate
student village. Typical of many of
Stanford's large housing complexes,
the units are organized into a series
of clusters arranged around lawns
and courtyards and linked by arbors.
The two- and three-story buildings
have their own formal organization within each cluster, thus personalizing
them. A postmodern interpretation of the Mission style unified the complex. Pastel hues, such as the sand-colored stucco walls, and ambiguous
details, such as circular windows with their modern references, lend the
wood-frame buildings a lightness and domestic feel.

Traditional Stanford elements, including red tile roofs, arcades,
metal railings, and fountains give a sense of belonging. The site originally
contained the Hacienda, an adobe winery built in 1875 by Peter Coutts and
later converted into a dairy barn before being transformed in the 1930s into
a faculty and student residence. The building was largely demolished to
make way for the new complex, though a fragment was preserved as a
backdrop to a semicircular pergola, while an old fountain created the focal
point for a courtyard. The white-brick Buttery, also a remnant of Coutts'
1875 farm, was restored and incorporated into the design. These touches
give the community special historical ties. The community was provided
with facilities to make it self-supporting, including laundry, music, computer,
game, and conference rooms, as well as a community center.

PART SEVEN

Restoration and Renewal: 1989-2000

125—

N

Rebirth of the Olmsted Plan

Two significant difficulties confronted Stanford's continued attainment of its ambitious goals as the institution entered the 1990s. First, a series of difficult financial negotiations with the federal government concerning its sponsored research programs created an atmosphere of apprehension about the future of funding for research in medicine, engineering, and the basic sciences that had fueled the tremendous growth at Stanford in both quality of programs and quantity of facilities. Second, in October 1989, the Loma Prieta earthquake caused tremendous damage and disruption to many key campus facilities in the core academic program areas, causing the closure of nearly half of the Main Quad buildings, the Stanford Museum, Green Library West, and many other teaching and research buildings. In all, more than one hundred buildings were damaged in some fashion. These two issues led to a prolonged and intensive period of priority review and planning activity. This period also allowed the opportunity to assess the future directions for the *restoration,* the *renewal,* and in some cases, the *replacement* of the existing core campus itself. This phase of activity continued into 1999, when both Green Library West and the Stanford Museum finally reopened. The rehabilitation of the last two unreinforced Main Quad structures culminated in the opening in 2002 of Wallenberg Hall, which houses the Stanford Center for Innovation in Learning (SCIL).

Initially, the university took a very cautious approach to rebuilding its damaged buildings, not unlike the response to the 1906 earthquake. Necessary repairs to student residences, which fortunately were modest, were completed expeditiously and large numbers of modular buildings were acquired to replace "temporarily" closed academic buildings so that no significant academic time was lost. Major repairs were delayed, in part, because of protracted negotiations with the Federal Emergency Management Agency (FEMA), which was to provide a significant percentage of the damage repair funding. After several years of wrangling over the eligibility of some of Stanford's damaged buildings, FEMA agreed to an overall "settlement" of approximately $40 million of the over $160 million total cost. Stanford was left with the daunting task of finding the remaining $120 million through a combination of borrowing and fundraising. Some of this "internal" funding was already being used to complete the beautiful restoration of Memorial Church in 1992 and several other smaller Main Quad structures.

The top leadership also changed during this crucial period, with Gerhard Casper arriving from the University of Chicago in 1992 to become Stanford's president. He immediately set out to reorganize the senior administration and to push strongly for settlements with the federal government on both the indirect cost and earthquake recovery issues. He also mandated that an approach to rebuilding be both efficient and thoughtful.

Previously, in 1989, the Stanford Board of Trustees had reconstituted its own Committee on Lands and Buildings, as well as established the position of university architect to oversee campus planning and design activities in response to the perceived mistakes of the 1970s and 1980s, such as the wrongful siting of buildings, the eclecticism of building designs, and the disjointed quality of the campus landscape. Following President Casper's direction, major new facilities were to be subject to international design competitions. This approach has as its twin objectives, to improve the design quality of future Stanford buildings to the level of its aspirations in its other key endeavors and to establish cross-institutional support for these designs through simultaneous engagement of trustees, administrators and end users in the selection process. In addition, significant internal efforts, led by then University Architect David J. Neuman, reconstructed many of the lost or hidden connective elements of the Olmsted plan, such as the creation of the Serra Mall, the enhancement of the athletics region, and the renewal of Palm Drive, Galvez Street, and Lasuen and Lomita Malls. This blend of both new and renovated historic buildings and the rehabilitated campus landscape has created a heightened level of acclaim, and sometimes controversy as a direct result. The major new projects exhibit a clear reference to their program and context, while at the same time, expressing the creative talents of their individual architects and landscape architects.

The hierarchy of campus plan, landscape, and architecture is intended to develop overall results that are "of Stanford," both of its heritage and its intended future.

111. Haas Center for Public Service

William Turnbull Associates, 1993

Haas Center for Public Service

One of William Turnbull's great design strengths was his small-scale residential work, which he translated here into a welcoming, "homelike" public services center for Stanford's undergraduate community volunteer groups. This pale yellow, three-story-with-attic, wood-frame building, has board-and-batten walls on the ground floor and horizontal siding above. It reflects the domestic scale of the surrounding buildings, which were a part of the first faculty residential neighborhood. Its details are simple yet bold, with tall and thin double-hung windows inserted into rectangular forms, including a stair tower, which serves as the main entry; it is wrapped by a surrounding porch. The asymmetrically organized composition encloses a courtyard for social gatherings. Inside the airy entry, an open staircase angles up to the second and third levels.

112. Cecil H. and Ida M. Green Earth Sciences Building

Anshen + Allen; Hargreaves Associates, landscape architects, 1993

After nearly ten years of planning and fundraising efforts and more than a century of thought, the first building to be designed according to the Near West Campus regional planning principles and design guidelines was constructed. It actually took the place of three small science and engineering buildings designed by Spencer in his low-rise modernist vocabulary of an earlier era. With the inclusion of the large pedestrian portal through the building, which spans the north-south axis, the design rigorously defines the strong notion of connection that is so seminal in Olmsted's original plan.

The Kresge Plaza, designed by Hargreaves Associates, is a large landscape terrace over the enlarged basement of the building. It interprets the geologic fault lines near the site, through a series of rock "outcroppings" that parallel their actual locations. It further symbolizes the nature of the research of many of the building's occupants and creates an important

Green Earth Sciences Building

connection with the Science and Engineering Quad to the north. While the building's surfaces are flattened in typical postmodern fashion, the exterior finishes are in keeping with traditional Stanford materials: sandstone-colored stucco with a variegated limestone base and trim elements and terra-cotta tile roofs.

113. Ralph Landau Center for Economics and Policy Research

Anshen + Allen; The SWA Group, landscape architects, 1994

Landau Center for Economics and Policy Research

This postmodern building is generally respectful of the historic character of the Stanford core campus in terms of planning, architecture, and landscape qualities. The general building massing is limited to three stories with conforming hipped tile roof, beige cast stone base and trim panels (some with archlike tracery in reference to the nearby Main Quad) and sandstone colored stucco, highlighted by dark green window frames and pale green glazing. The interior court opens to the west to the Memorial Auditorium/Tanner Fountain area in a complementary relationship.

114. Charles B. Thornton Center for Engineering Management

Tanner, Leddy, Maytum, Stacy; Peter Walker/William Johnson and Partners, landscape architects, 1994

Thornton Center for Engineering Management

Located next to Santa Teresa Street at the southern boundary of the sciences and engineering area, the building has been designed as a southern gateway to the Terman Engineering Center. A two-story, open-air portal frames the view of the original building and the large (redesigned) fountain courtyard to form an inviting, major entry point. The AIA-awarding-winning building has been designed to define the third side of the courtyard, and further complements the adjacent James Gibbons oak grove, which is linked by a sliding copper-clad door to allow indoor-outdoor social functions. The exterior materials of the center extend the character of the original Terman building without mere mimicry in neomodernist severity. The simple beige stucco walls are covered by a large tile-clad shed roof drawn from the much larger Terman structure, with the ridge side of the building featuring north-facing clerestory windows and rich copper cladding. The entire Terman courtyard and fountain were redesigned by Peter Walker to better enhance the completed complex.

115. William Gates Computer Science Building

Robert A. M. Stern and Partners; Sebastian & Associates, landscape architects, 1996

William Gates Computer Science Building

The siting and form of the building deviate dramatically from the 1987 Near West Campus Plan; it called for actual closure of the Serra axis with a pair of buildings forming an exedra. This would have repeated the same mistakes made with earlier buildings sited over all of the other prominent Olmsted axes, such as Meyer Library and Durand over Escondido, Mitchell over Lomita, and Braun and Littlefield over Lasuen. Fortunately, its revised siting emphasizes the prominence of the location at the intersection of what has become the Serra Mall and the north-south axis, which are both high-use pedestrian and bicycle corridors. The architectural references are primarily to the Main Quad in general forms, materials, and colors interpreted in a prominent and sophisticated postmodern fashion. Its L shape shelters a well-landscaped courtyard with many mature trees, either preserved on-site or transplanted to give this tall structure an immediate sense of campuswide scale.

116. Paul Allen Center for Integrated Systems Addition

Antoine Predock; Sebastian & Associates, landscape architects, 1995

This project represents the first outcome of an international design competition at Stanford under President Casper's administration. The challenge of a complex program on a very tight site as an addition to a mildly eccentric, postmodern structure was taken by four design teams: Predock; Edward L. Barnes; Moore, Ruble, Yudell; and Esherick Homsey Dodge and Davis, each of which produced unique responses. The selected design contrasts the new addition with the existing architectural character of the older CIS

Paul Allen Center for Integrated Systems

structure. Yet through its proportions, massing, and roofline, the new design complements the original CIS building, as well as its other neighbors. The AIA-award-winning design draws the complete CIS/CISX building into the Stanford main campus architectural vocabulary in a strong manner. The exterior finishes are of Indian sandstone veneer, black metal window frames with clear glazing, and oxidizing copper-shingled roofing which sits above a clerestory glazing line to create the impression that the roof is floating above the walls, especially at night. The arch of the main entry at Serra Mall is proportioned like the Main Quad arches, from which it is visible. A carefully landscaped interior atrium not only allows natural light into all sides of the interior but also is formed on one side by a glass wall into the older building's clean room functions.

117. William R. Hewlett and David Packard Science and Engineering Quad

Pei Cobb Freed and Partners; Olin Partnership, landscape architects, 1995–1999

As Stanford began its second century, the importance of teaching and research in the sciences and engineering was reaffirmed by a renewed commitment to the development of facilities reflecting the character and caliber of the work being done in these fields. The Hewlett and Packard Science and Engineering Quad was built directly from the stalled Near West Campus Plan, energizing and extending that effort. Significantly, the vast majority of funding for this $120 million project came from two of Stanford's most successful

William R. Hewlett and David Packard Science and Engineering Quad (looking east to Main Quad)

engineering graduates, William R. Hewlett and David Packard, whose corporation flourished next to their alma mater in the Stanford Research Park.

This total project provides the David Packard Electrical Engineering building; the Gordon and Betty Moore Materials Research building; the William R. Hewlett Teaching Center; and a replacement Statistics building. The new buildings are integral to the creation of a new Science and Engineering Quad, partially enclosed with freestanding metal arcades, and other landscape and circulation features, the design of which draws heavily on the original Olmsted-Stanford campus plan of 1888.

The overall design of the Hewlett and Packard Science and Engineering Quad, also the result of an invited design competition won by Freed and Olin, relies on use of a common architectural and landscape vocabulary for the new Sequoia Hall, Moore building, and Packard building. Features include attached arcades and deeply recessed windows with French limestone veneer and precast concrete on the first level. Clay tile roofs, stucco walls with granite-clad bases, and copper eaves and other trim are also part of the overall vocabulary. In contrast, the Hewlett Teaching Center and main stair tower of the Packard Electrical Engineering building punctuate the entry to the quad complex. Clad in silver-painted metal and clear glass, they literally point the way into the new Quad in the same fashion as the original Memorial Arch led to the Main Quad a century ago. The freestanding arcades framing the new Quad itself are constructed of steel, stone, and translucent fabric roofing, with the curving shape springing from the entry curve of the teaching center. Overall, the composition is a stirring completion of Olmsted's and the Stanfords' original intent.

OPPOSITE: *William R. Hewlett Teaching Center and David Packard Electrical Engineering*

David Packard Electrical Engineering This very contextual building is designed to complete the area bounded by the Gates Computer Sciences building and the Allen Center for Integrated Systems. The building is three stories tall and has a full basement with an elongated plan layout intended to enhance communication among faculty and students in all three programmatically related buildings. A prominent interior feature of the building is an atrium with a large skylight, which provides natural light to all levels of the building. A dramatic eastern entry stair tower "prow" and an integrated arcade set the theme for the freestanding arcades extending to the south into the new Quad, while its ground-floor café opens to the plaza area, which houses a watertable by Maya Lin.

Gordon and Betty Moore Materials Research This building houses most of the facilities of the Laboratory for Advanced Materials (LAM) and of the Center for Materials Research (CMR)-laboratories which are dedicated to research into the synthesis, understanding, and applications of advanced materials, and to the education of graduate students from various scientific and engineering disciplines. The structure, connected to the renovated McCullough Building, is in keeping with the architectural vocabulary of the other quad buildings, which is based on that of the Main Quad. Its siting and its integrated arcade frame the recreated palm-lined Olmstedian connection between the Hewlett and Packard Science and Engineering Quad and the Main Quad. This became possible with the demolition of the physics teaching facility ("the Tank"), which had blocked this intended pedestrian connection.

Sequoia Hall This building houses the Statistics Department and contains offices for faculty, students, and staff; a computer classroom; a lounge; a small library; a classroom; and ancillary spaces. This corner building, sited at the juncture of Serra and Lomita Malls, is in line with the Main Quad buildings to the east and is companion to the Thomas Welton Stanford Art Gallery on the other side of the Main Quad. A south courtyard is created between the building and Varian to provide a gathering space and a buffer for the prominent student traffic to the Hewlett Teaching Center.

William R. Hewlett Teaching Center

William R. Hewlett Teaching Center This dynamic building houses the classrooms and lecture halls used in undergraduate physics, chemistry, and biology lectures, at a size and configuration allowing a wide variety of uses. The two lecture halls are connected to a demonstration, preparation, and storage area by two revolving-turntable lecture stages. The lecture halls are designed to support instructional technology as well as TV production and remote transmission. The building serves as the gateway to the Hewlett and Packard Quad from Palm Drive and Serra Mall and interacts dramatically with the adjacent Packard Electrical Engineering's main stairway "prow." The shape and mass of this building create contrast, as well as balance for the other buildings in the region. The exterior material reflects this contrast, as the curved west facade is sheathed in coated metal, while the remaining walls are of either the same French limestone used on other Quad buildings, which is reminiscent of the nearby Main Quad's sandstone in color and texture and buff, or integrally colored stucco.

Hewlett and Packard Quad The new Quad and associated landscaping serve as the unifying focus of this region. The quad provides places to sit, study, and socialize for all the members of the academic community. The landscape concept of four prominent lawn panels surrounded by Italian stone pines defines the circulation pattern through the area. The organization of the quad is based on the original plan for the campus. The site is bordered and linked by freestanding arcades. They are constructed of steel and covered in translucent fabric, which is uplit at night to create a striking, curved enclosure of the courtyard space. Small pavilions, which house black granite fountains designed by John Wong of the SWA Group, are located at entry points to the main courtyard.

118. Knight Building

Skidmore, Owings, and Merrill; The SWA Group, landscape architects, 1999

This building, which attaches to the Littlefield Center, completes several important tasks at the same time. First, it turns Littlefield away from the Oval area toward the mass of the older Graduate School of Business building and forms a strong courtyard link with that structure, both physically and programmatically. This is done with the intervening landscaped plaza between the two buildings, which creates a center of activity between them. Second, it attempts to stylistically mediate between the two structures with differing elevations to the south (toward the Graduate School of Business's modernism) and to the north (in contemporary concert with Littlefield's postmodernism). Third, it is a strong statement on its own of basic neomodernist design principles actively responding to site and program needs while recognizing the lessons of the recent past to actively engage the context of the campus itself. Limestone as used on other recent Stanford buildings, such as the nearby Ford Center, and other materials and colors in harmony with the traditional campus palette assist this modestly sized building to complete its tasks in a successful fashion.

Knight Building

119. Arrillaga Family Sports Center

Hoover Associates; The SWA Group, landscape architects, 1993

This multipurpose building provides space for athletic administration, intercollegiate sports, recreation activities, and the Stanford sports hall of fame. Developed by the donor, John Arrillaga, the three-story tilt-up concrete structure follows the general guidelines of the central campus material and color palette and, with its siting and strong landscaping, creates a coherent relationship with the surrounding athletic complex; it also

Arrillaga Family Sports Center

initiates a new quadrangle built around this theme. This development of order within the athletics area has continued from this point to create a positive interaction with the central campus through the Ford Quad; it allows a careful renewal and expansion of sports facilities that are not only state-of-the-art but also accessible to the general campus community on a spectator or participant basis.

120. Taube Tennis Center

ELS/Elbasani–Logan; The SWA Group, landscape architects, 1997

This expansion of the Milton Pflueger-designed tennis stadium from 1983 incorporates an exuberance for the sport of tennis at Stanford, where so many NCAA championship teams have been fostered. Most notable is the sunken indoor court, which tucks under the east bleachers in part and whose remaining width is covered by a semicircular, fabric-covered roof. Additional improvements to the existing facilities have created one of the finest collegiate tennis centers anywhere.

Taube Tennis Center

121. Avery Aquatic Center

ELS/Elbasani–Logan, The SWA Group, landscape architects, 1999

This expansion of the former deGuerre pools (#82) includes the Maas Diving Center, the Belardi Pool (Olympic-size), the Avery Stadium Pool, and expanded lockers to create one of the most comprehensive outdoor aquatic facilities in collegiate sports.

Avery Aquatic Center

122. Kimball Hall

Backen, Arrigoni & Ross; Ken Kay Associates, landscape architects, 1991

Kimball Hall

Because of the increasing shortage of rental housing in the area around Stanford, due to the tremendous boom in Silicon Valley's economic growth, as well as the continuing need to compete with peer universities for the best undergraduate students, Stanford prioritized the building (and renovation) of significant student housing during this period. One such effort included the replacement of the "trailer park," known as Manzanita Park, which had existed since the late 1960s as "temporary" student housing, through a series of student housing projects of strong presence.

Kimball Hall, adjacent to Branner Hall, was the first phase of the replacement of the Manzanita Park trailers with a permanent facility. The H-shaped undergraduate dorm relates to the form of Branner, but its architecture returns to a postmodern reference of "top, middle, and base" layering, which is achieved successfully despite its mere three-story height. This success is attributable to excellent detailing in its roof over-hang, hand-wrought copper gutters and downpipes, cast-stone sills, and careful coloration of its stucco facades. In short, the tradition of Bakewell and Brown's eclecticism at Stanford is continued with aplomb.

123. Lantana and Castaño Halls

Fisher-Friedman Associates; The SWA Group, landscape architects, 1992

Lantana and Castaño Halls

The second phase of the Manzanita Park replacement consisted of two linked undergraduate dorms forming the eastern edge of what will become a residential quadrangle. Even more postmodern than Kimball, these buildings, and their companion dining hall, draw their inspiration from the Italianate "towers" of Toyon Hall. The resulting collision of this modest verticality, especially in relationship to the nearby Hoover Tower, creates a particularly unique sense of a Stanford-related environment, which when coupled with the strong landscape elements of pergolas and quadlike setting is quite striking.

124. Schwab Residential Learning Center

Legorreta Arquitectos/The Steinberg Group; Peter Walker and Partners, landscape architects, 1997

The project has 280 studio apartment units with shared kitchen-dining areas. Other spaces include group study rooms, central kitchen-dining areas, lounges, exercise rooms, laundries, offices, and other common areas. These are used by 220 students in the Graduate School of Business and 60 visiting executives for continued learning during the normal academic year, and by 280 participants in summer executive programs during that season.

The design concept for this project is based on the traditional *hacienda,* just as other earlier Stanford residential buildings, such as Lagunita Court, are related to their interior courtyards. In this instance, four court-yards organize the site design with an arrival palm court and an archetypal column court for the dining and support facilities, along with two others of distinct characteristics (fountain and pines) for each of the two residential areas. Although the residential unit plans themselves are all exactly similar,

Schwab Residential Center

they are organized in distinctive building forms, not only to surround the landscaped courts but also to provide individuality in the unit's orientation and outside views. While the overall buildings range from one to four stories in an architectural vocabulary of materials and fenestration patterns strongly derived from the existing Stanford central campus palette, a simple entry tower evokes the directly surrounding neighbors of Toyon, Lantana and Castaño Halls. Perimeter coloring is in the earth tones of the nearby structures, and bold colors (yellow, purple, blue, and terra-cotta) accent the interior courtyards, adding interest and complementing the strong land-scape theme of the project.

125. Lyman Residential Center *Tanner Leddy Maytum Stacy; Hargreaves Associates, landscape architects, 1997–1998*

The AIA award-winning design concept for the Lyman Residential Center is based strongly on the narrow site and clear ordering of the major building elements: the commons building around a large oak tree as a organizing structure; a semicircular cluster of four-story apartments to the south; and a gently curved line of four-story apartment units extending to the north. The exterior skin of the apartments is primarily stucco and cement board, with a panelized appearance punctuated by glazed areas and a copper-clad "roof" to screen the mechanical equipment. Algerian red metal sunscreens surround the building on the south and west elevations, adding solar

Lyman Residential Center

protection and creating another layer of depth to the otherwise flat elevations. The commons area is a dramatic tile-roofed circle-in-a-square structure, surrounding a heritage oak tree and punctuated by corner skylight
towers built of exposed concrete-aggregate masonry. Heavy landscaping
surrounds the project with regional plantings in colors and patterns coordinated with the buildings. The residential units are named for Richard W.
Lyman, the university's seventh president (1970–80), and the commons
building for his wife, Jing.

126. Escondido Village Studios I–IV

Solomon ETC; The SWA Group, landscape architects, 2000–2003

Escondido Village Studio I

This project of two pairs of buildings
represents the latest in providing
affordable, on-campus housing for
graduate students by providing
"infill" contextually designed studio
apartments that relate to their surroundings with the minimum of intru-
sion into this Mumford-inspired
environs. Built in two successive
phases of two buildings each, the sec-
ond pair not only are the most successful from a site planning and aesthetic
perspective, but also incorporate major improvements in user amenities.

127. Medical School Lab Surge/Lucas Magnetic Spectroscopy Center *Stone, Marriccini, Patterson, 1992*

Medical School Lab Surge/Lucas Center

This project started as two buildings that for a variety of reasons became one structure, which still shows its origins. The major component (MSLS) developed a strong postmodern relationship to the nearby E. D. Stone complex, while the smaller Lucas Center exhibits a curvilinear form that is somewhat related to the functional areas within its EIFS walls. Overall the project creates an appropriate entry to the drama of the Stone complex and its fountain courtyard.

128. Blake Wilbur Clinic *Marshall Erdman & Associates, 1993*

This design-build facility draws its modest design inspiration from the nearby Packard Children's Hospital and its postmodern Stanford campus references. It houses many of the Stanford Hospital's outpatient clinics and treatment facilites.

129. Psychiatry and Human Behavior Building

Bobrow / Thomas Associates; Burton & Spitz, landscape architects, 1993

Psychiatry and Human Behavior Building

This building is intended to be the start of a psychiatry research center that was to include an inpatient hospital and a children's clinic. These projects have not as yet been built, so this departmental office-research facility and medical clinic stands remote from its related clinical and academic buildings in the Stanford University Medical Center. The overall design of the building, including the linear water feature in the entry courtyard, is inspired by the Louis Kahn-designed Salk Center in La Jolla, California. Following the Medical Center design guidelines, the building's exterior colors and details draw on both the nearby Packard Children's Hospital and the Hoover Pavilion in terms of forms, details, and colors. The powerful landscape treatment shields the occupants from nearby busy streets and vice versa.

130. Center for Clinical Sciences Research

Sir Norman Foster and Partners/ Fong and Chan; Peter Walker and Partners, landscape architects, 1999–2000

Center for Clinical Sciences Research, interior courtyard

The design concept of this center is based generally on the following three principles: strong architectural and landscape response to context, especially the E. D. Stone complex; straightforward and flexible organization of both floor plans and massing; and emphasis on the use of natural day light, with solar control wherever required. The four-story buildings are organized as two identical linear elements composed of labs, support space, and offices, which face one another across a covered outdoor courtyard. There is also a basement, housing the anatomy program and building support areas, which is daylit through a depressed landscaped area within the courtyard. Open stairs and glass-enclosed elevators within the courtyard emphasize the openness of the plan, as well as the collegiality of the research programs that are housed in the center.

The structure is of cast-in-place concrete with the majority of the skin of the building made of precast concrete and metal/glass curtain wall shaded by two prominent trellis structures made of painted steel and unpainted aluminum. These materials, as well as the building's general massing and height, build on, and dramatically enhance, the context of the surrounding buildings, the Beckman Center, the Medical School Lab Surge/Lucas Center, and, especially, the E. D. Stone complex. The overall design is one of simplicity of structural order and use of materials and refinement of site work and details of construction.

Center for Clinical Sciences Research

131. Center for Cancer Treatment and Prevention/Ambulatory Care Pavilion

Bobrow/Thomas Associates; Pamela Burton and Peter Walker and Partners, landscape architects, 2000–2003

Center for Cancer Treatment and Prevention/Ambulatory Care Pavilion

This recent project was designed to advance the state of cancer prevention and treatment, as well as provide state-of-the-art outpatient surgery facilities. The site was chosen because of its direct relationship to the Packard Hospital, the Stanford Hospital, and the Blake-Wilbur Clinic, as well as its proximity to utilities and patient parking. Its massing and material palette are related to its programs and balance with the form of the Center for Clinical Sciences Research, which is directly to the west. A unique feature is the use of the extension of the upper level to create a covered patient drop-off zone with welcoming landscape features.

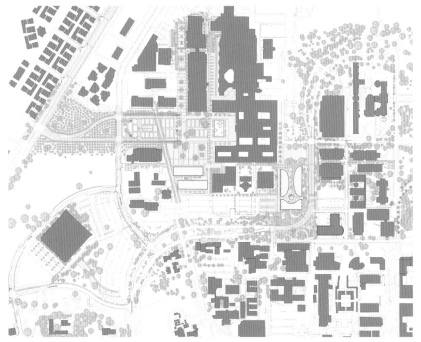

Medical Center Area Plan, 1999; Peter Walker and Partners with the University Architect/Planning Office

Into the Next Millenium: 2001-2005

149

1

1

To Jasper Ridge
Biological Preserve

147

To Redwood Shores

141

132

146

143

134

139

151

135

142

133

136

N

A New Emphasis on Sustainability

At the beginning of the new century, Stanford was completing a cycle of restoration and renewal of many of its historic structures, most of which had been damaged severely by the 1989 Loma Prieta earthquake. With the opening of Wallenberg Hall (Building 160), located along the front of the Main Quad, Stanford not only finished the massive, decade-long effort to refurbish its historic academic core, but also demonstrated how a hundred-year-old structure could be recycled for its fourth major reuse: since its completion in 1900, the building had been transformed from a library to a law school to the political science department, and now serves as a digital learning center. As this period of recovery neared completion (with only six unreinforced masonry structures now remaining to be strengthened), in 1999, Stanford was recognized with the Governor's Historic Preservation Award and in 2000 received the National Preservation Honor Award. In addition to its restoration efforts, the university also continued to focus its attention on expanding its campus, and major land use planning efforts were underway in order to allow the university to develop further.

Two of these complex planning activities are most noteworthy: the renewal of the Stanford General Use Permit with Santa Clara County, and the entitlement of a series of projects along the western boundary of the campus, generally known as Stanford West, located mainly in the City of Palo Alto. These endeavors took many years of careful thinking, well-orchestrated public outreach, and difficult and skillful negotiations. As a result of the negotiations, Stanford is allowed to continue to expand physically to meet its academic and support activity objectives, while its impacts on the surrounding communities are recognized and mitigated. A significant series of expensive compensations and a set of clear land use constraints for the future were agreed upon, including a growth boundary along the southern edge of the developed campus, generally contiguous with Junipero Serra Boulevard, that disallows the golf course and lower foothills from being used for any significant development for the next twenty years or more.

All of these planning efforts reinforced several of Stanford's major trends in planning and development over the previous decade, especially the practices of the use of infill site planning and replacement of existing outmoded and/or low-density facilities including surface parking lots. To offset the loss of parking space while infilling with new buildings occupied by more faculty, staff, and students, Stanford not only built large parking garages, but also aggressively pursued its successful programs in transportation demand management, including a new emphasis on the use of the existing commuter rail system (CALTRAIN). In addition, more graduate student housing was rapidly constructed in Escondido Village, while a new development of apartments in the Stanford West project was reprioritized for internal use by faculty and staff.

Sustainability also took on renewed meaning at Stanford with increased emphasis on limiting the energy use in new structures and on maintaining environmentally sensitive approaches to all construction. Such well-established practices as on-site management of storm water, protection of heritage trees, development of additional bicycle and pedestrian facilities, and enhancements to the central cogeneration facilities were taken on with new vigor. While not requiring Leadership in Energy and Environmental Design (LEED) certification of its new buildings, Stanford developed its own comprehensive standards to be pursued with each project. All of these activities led to Santa Clara County's certification of Stanford University as a "green" organization in 2004. Many of Stanford's buildings during this period, from the Clark Center to the Sun Field Station to the Carnegie Institution of Washington, clearly note this trend toward sustainability, echoing in their own fashions the core principles of passive solar design of the original Main Quad buildings from more than a century earlier.

132. Frances C. Arrillaga Alumni Center

Hoover Associates; The SWA Group, landscape architects, 2000-2002

Frances C. Arrillaga Alumni Center

Dedicated in memory of a Stanford alumna by her family, this multipurpose building houses both the Offices of Development and the Stanford Alumni Association. The center also provides extensive conference facilities, a major ballroom, and food services. Events hosted range from lectures, luncheons, dinners, continued learning activities, and pre- and post-athletic gatherings to private parties and wedding receptions. Its site, formerly occupied by Galvez House and the university's second central plant (one-time home of the Stanford Band and well-known as "The Band Shak"), was chosen for its proximity to the core academic and athletics regions, as well as its location on Galvez Street, the most highly public trafficked entry to the campus. This infill site to a large degree influenced the "L" shape of the building, with its public face toward Galvez Street and Campus Drive. The interior of the site plan faces the adjacent wooded bank of Frost Amphitheater, and creates a nearly enclosed space for a dramatic outdoor garden, which features various California native plant species and includes a cascading fountain and terrace.

Student Services Center

133. Student Services Center

> *Cody Anderson Wasney (CAW) Architects; The SWA Group, landscape architects, 2000–2002*

Sited on the southeastern end of Salvatierra Mall, next to Campus Drive East, the building is intended to complement the nearby Haas Center for Public Service, as well as the adjacent Owen, Rogers, and Mariposa houses, which date to the late-nineteenth century, when they were among the first faculty homes sited on the campus. Its size, however, makes this difficult to accomplish, despite the architectural gestures in form and materials. As the surrounding landscape matures, it will aid in fitting this relatively large structure into its environs.

In addition to accommodating a massive redwood tree to the rear of the site, the building is noteworthy for its porches, which were made fully accessible without resorting to an overt ramp. This is especially important as a primary occupant is the Student Disability Resource Center, along with the Career Development Center.

134. James H. Clark Center for Biosciences and Bioengineering

> *Foster and Partners/MBT Architecture; Peter Walker and Partners, landscape architects, 2000–2003*

One of the most spectacular buildings ever to be developed at Stanford, the award-winning Clark Center sprang from a faculty-based initiative (Bio-X) directed toward interdisciplinary research at the highest levels in bio-sciences and bioengineering. The building houses Stanford faculty from a multitude of departments, as well as visiting faculty and postdoctoral fellows from around the world. The infill site was chosen to be central to faculty and students in both the medical center and the core academic campus, including the existing and future buildings surrounding the Hewlett and Packard Science and Engineering Quad. The Clark Center's open tripartite plan is intended to serve as a "hinge" between these two regions, and to facilitate pedestrian traffic through, rather than around, the structure. Its generally inward-facing orientation is meant to enhance the pedestrians' experience (and curiosity), as well as to make researchers in all parts of the building aware of the high activity level in the center. The building features two food service facilities that are open to the public, the first-level cafeteria and the third-level café. In addition, a major conference room is located beneath the central, circular court, which is also used for outdoor events and dining. Sustainability is highlighted in the shaded central courtyard, which is open to gentle breezes, while the system of outdoor walkways on all floors of the building serves as sunshades and reduces the interior conditioned volume by approximately fifteen percent, thus saving both capital and operating costs. The massing, materials, and landscape are meant to "knit" the beaux-arts traditions of the Richardsonian Main Quad to the modernity of E. D. Stone's massive medical center complex. All in all, a masterful resolution of a complex set of program, site and design issues is evident in the internationally acclaimed Clark Center.

James H. Clark Center for Biosciences and Bioengineering

135. Escondido Village: Studios V-VI

Solomon ETC; The SWA Group, landscape architects, 2001–2003

Escondido Village: Studios V-VI

Following the completion of the first two building phases of the Escondido Village studio apartments for graduate students (#126, Studios I–IV), the university decided to continue the program in a more comprehensive and better-funded fashion with another pair of studio apartment buildings that have additional amenities in the individual apartments and include common areas, such as a student lounge and computer learning center. Architect Daniel Solomon and landscape architect John Wong of the SWA Group worked together once again and, learning from experience in the previous two phases, produced results that are the best of these efforts to date in terms of both architectural and landscape character. Though there remain some obvious clashes in scale between these long four-story structures and their older, smaller neighbors, the juxtaposition (and the protection of mature existing landscape) results in a complementary addition to the Escondido Village milieu.

136. Allene G. Vaden Health Center

Hawley Peterson Snyder Architects; Antonia Bava, landscape architects, 2001–2003

Allene G. Vaden Health Center

Built as a larger and more flexible student health facility directly next to the Cowell Health Center (#79) (demolished upon completion of the Vaden building), the new structure is a strong, public presence along Campus Drive East. Its front entry and lovely gardens adjoin a campus shuttle bus stop, promoting welcoming and easy access to a building whose use is more related to personal counseling and health promotion than to the Cowell Health Center's traditional "infirmary" environment. The material palette and the architectural form are intended to identify with the traditions of Stanford, including Antoine Predock's Paul Allen Center (#116), but its interiors speak of contemporary care for today's students in a manner similar to many of the better health care clinics in the surrounding communities.

Leslie Sun Biological Field Station

137. Leslie Sun Biological Field Station

Rob Wellington Quigley Architects, 2001–2003

For many years, the Jasper Ridge Biological Preserve (JRBP) was served by a collection of temporary and residual structures remaining from the time it was a publicly accessible park, prior to its designation as a biological preserve. These facilities served researchers, students, visitors, and local docents as best they could. After a successful and responsive development campaign, Stanford decided to reward the perseverance of all involved with the dramatic success of the Preserve's work by allowing a new entirely sustainable structure to be designed and built. From siting and material considerations to active and passive solar systems to rainwater collection, the Sun Station is truly "green" from top to bottom so that its power meter spins in reverse. Located several miles away from the core campus, it was free from the sandstone and tile traditions that rightly provoke self-consciousness in terms of design and therefore stands on its own environmental tenets. It was honored by the AIA Committee on the Environment (COTE) as one of the top ten green projects for 2005.

138. Parking Structure No. 4

Watry Associates; Peter Walker and Partners, landscape architects, 2001–03

No other Stanford parking structures have been mentioned in this guide because, despite valiant efforts in some cases to mitigate their necessary presence, their aesthetic results have been disappointing. Parking Structure No. 4 is worth noting, however, because its construction has created, at long last, a beautiful entry to the Stanford University Medical Center and its long-suffering E. D. Stone and Thomas Church–designed (Moorish-inspired)

Parking Structure No. 4

front entry fountain and plaza. Watry and Walker accomplish this through two significant and expensive design decisions—they put the cars underground and covered them with a beautiful garden. The result is spectacular, changing the sense of arrival at this major medical center completely from a forgotten wasteland to a memorable garden. At last there is an entryway worthy of the institution itself and the namesakes for the main drive, the Pasteurs. In the best tradition of Le Nôtre, Walker's garden design has honored the Pasteurs, Stanford, and everyone's quest for the best in health care.

139. Boyd & Jill Smith Family Stadium, Steuber Rugby Stadium, Doyle Family Rugby Clubhouse, and Maloney Field

Hoover Associates; The SWA Group, landscape architects, 2001–2003

Boyd & Jill Smith Family Stadium with Field Hockey in background

This series of major improvements to these sports facilities in the athletics region of the campus carefully followed the American Society of Landscape Architects (ASLA) award-winning plan, with each facility adding to the careful organization and user-friendly atmosphere of the area. Landscaped pathways accommodate both pedestrians and bicyclists, many of whom commute daily through this region from next-door Palo Alto. The stadiums themselves are state-of-the-art, yet blend into, and contribute to, the overall ambiance of the athletics complex and the campus as a whole. The continuity of materials and workmanship is unique for such facilities and represents a dedication to the principles of a coherent and functional, yet aesthetic, campus environment. It is a tribute to the donors, designers, and administrators who have seen this ten-year plan to improve facilities for softball, rugby, soccer, and lacrosse to completion.

Carnegie Foundation for the Advancement of Teaching

140. Carnegie Foundation for the Advancement of Teaching

Seidel-Holzman Architects; Royston Hanamoto Alley and Abey, landscape architects, 2001–2003

Joining a small group of Stanford-related research centers in the area adjoining the Stanford Golf Course facilities, the Carnegie Foundation was built only after a lengthy public process of determining whether this type of "think tank" use could continue in this setting, despite the fact that the adjacent Center for the Advanced Study in the Behavioral Sciences (#56) had existed successfully in this location for nearly fifty years. Santa Clara County eventually approved the plan, and the resulting architecture and landscape is an excellent product of the creative dynamic of the program and the site. The building nestles into difficult slope conditions, while protecting heritage trees, local grasslands, historic barns, and overall viewsheds. The building's solar orientation, roof overhangs, and (somewhat) earth-sheltered interior conditions, along with the general use of other passive solar and local material principles, are all in response to the sympathetic resolution of a difficult site/program problem.

141. Lorry I. Lokey Laboratory for Chemistry and Biological Sciences

Ellenzweig Associates; Sebastian & Associates, landscape architects, 2002–2004

"An aggressive set of program requirements meet a very tight site" may be the simple description of an overall design result that is both commendable and somewhat controversial at the same time. For many years, the Seeley

Lorry I. Lokey Laboratory for Chemistry and Biological Sciences

G. Mudd Chemistry Building (#54) was slated for future expansion by an addition to the north, which would connect to an under-used balcony level. The new building connects quite well, especially given the change in floor-to-floor heights dictated by current mechanical/ventilation system needs. However, from some directions it appears to overwhelm the site. This is not the fault of the designers, as both architects and landscape architects have done their best to mitigate a large program on such a narrow site. When viewed from the medical center side of Campus Drive, the building appears well adapted to a complex context of increasing density, including its connective multi-level pedestrian walkways and architectural vocabulary. (Note that the giant bamboo between these buildings repeats the theme along the pedestrian axis linking this complex to the Center for Clinical Sciences Research (#130) and the Lucas Center Expansion (#149). It is a worthy response to both the challenge and opportunity of uniting the central campus with the medical center and with the Clark Center.

142. Graduate Student Community Center

Hoover Associates, 2003–2004

In response to the increased number of graduate students living on campus, in general, and to the initial infill projects of the Escondido Village Studios I–II (#126) in particular, Stanford moved forward with the concept of developing a community center for graduate students. This facility provides everything from child care and meeting rooms to yoga training and nighttime entertainment in a central and welcoming setting.

143. Roscoe Maples Pavilion Expansion

Hoover Associates with HOK Sport, Inc.; The SWA Group, landscape architects, 2002–2005

In order to accommodate the requirements of the Americans with Disabilities Act, to add more locker facilities and to provide spectator amenities such as a lobby and expanded concessions and restrooms, the Department of Athletics, Physical Education and Recreation determined to expand the existing Maples Pavilion. The original 1957 design by John Carl

Roscoe Maples Pavilion Expansion

Warnecke (#81) seemed to be completely self-contained and resolute. After significant study, however, the concept of expanding the amenities of the structure, rather than the seating capacity, was quite achievable; and, in fact, very sustainable in principle, through the design of a naturally ventilated, covered "donut" of support space around the original structure. This design solution provides basic facilities such as concessions and restrooms, as well as increased (subterranean) areas for lockers for both men's and women's basketball and volleyball teams. The provision facilities for both genders responds to Federal mandates and has fostered a remarkably successful intercollegiate program in all sports, including basketball and volleyball, both housed in Maples. The result is a unique structure that both respects its (now historic) past, as well as looks to its (sustainable) future.

144. Carnegie Institution of Washington Expansion

Esherick Homsey Dodge and Davis; Ron Lutsko Associates, landscape architects, 2002–2004

This addition to the Carnegie Institution (#34), established on the Stanford campus in 1929, represents a major commitment to sustainable principles in design, as well as a renewal of the strong relationship of this institution to Stanford's Biology Department. The building itself utilized the best elements in passive solar design, while experimenting with the concepts of thermal storage in a contemporary office environment, as well as night-sky roofing, seasonal solar shading, and indigenous planting. It received a 2005 Honor Award from the San Francisco Chapter of the AIA.

Carnegie Institution of Washington Expansion

145. Nora Suppes Building

Page and Turnbull Architects; The SWA Group, landscape architects, 2003–2005

Nora Suppes Building

This building completes the unique complex of small buildings devoted to research into language (Center for Study of Language and Information—CSLI) and learning (Education Program for Gifted Youth—EPGY) by forming a central courtyard to bring all of the occupants together around a carefully landscaped space—a common theme at Stanford. The new building utilizes passive solar design principles that are evident in Stanford's original Main Quad, including outdoor walkways, deep roof overhangs, and operable windows, while general colors and materials also reference this historic precedent.

146. Arrillaga Family Recreation Center

Hoover Associates; The SWA Group, landscape architects, 2003–2005

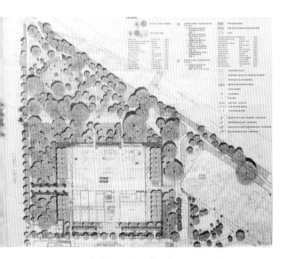

Arrillaga Family Recreation Center

After a study showed that it was infeasible to re-use the historic structure for the new and expanded program, the Board of Trustees decided to replace the Bakewell and Brown–designed Encina Gym (#31) with a new recreation center, donated and built by one of Stanford's most generous donors. The new structure respects the siting and arrangement of the remaining earlier buildings (#31), the Ford Center (#107), and the associated Ford Quad. Its main entry and architectural details reflect the general relationship to the Ford Center and Burnham Pavilion, while its secondary elevation respects the heritage oak grove facing north toward Campus Drive. In addition, its siting is easily accessible from the large majority of both graduate and undergraduate student housing.

147. Stanford University Rowing and Sailing Center: Morrison Boat House

Hoover Associates, 2003–2004

This facility replaces inadequate facilities at its open-water location in Redwood Shores with an enlarged and significantly enhanced set of facilities. The new two-story boathouse has lower-level accommodations for both men's and women's crew and sailing, while the second level has locker areas, exercise facilities, and large function room.

148. Stanford Auxiliary Library III

MBT Architecture; Smith & Smith, landscape architects, 2002–2004

Stanford Auxiliary Library III

While Stanford has built and operated facilities removed from the main campus, such as the Hopkins Marine Station in Monterey and the Jasper Ridge Biological Preserve in the Stanford foothills, the site of these operations was dictated by the need to be adjacent to natural environments required for biological studies. With the construction of the Stanford Auxiliary Library III (SAL III) in Livermore, forty-five miles from the campus, the off-site rationale has been redefined further to incorporate local land values and future ease of expansion. The academic growth boundary imposed by Santa Clara County in 2000 and spiraling land values in the vicinity of the campus have influenced the decision to develop some of Stanford's support facilities at some distance from the central campus. The first of these facilities is the handsome SAL III structure, which houses little-used library volumes. A daily shuttle to the main campus links this site with the main library facilities on campus so that books can be retrieved easily as needed by faculty and students.

149. Lucas Center Expansion

MBT Architecture; Bruce Jett, landscape architect, 2003–2005

Lucas Center Expansion

This is a remarkable facility, despite being nearly entirely underground. It fulfills the program requirements of the Department of Radiological Sciences, as well as completes a vital portion of the medical center region plan by contributing carefully designed site improvements at grade level. It also helps to resolve pedestrian access issues created by the original building's loading and drop-off areas interface. An eye-catching lightwell with giant bamboo plantings delves into this three-story deep structure. The relationship of the interior spaces to the lightwell and to passersby at grade create a novel, yet essential relationship to the general campus itself, especially the nearby Center for Clinical Sciences Research (#130). This project is a true integration of site planning, landscape, and architecture at its highest (and physically lowest) level.

150. Stanford West Development: Apartments and Senior Living, Shopping Center Additions, and Infrastructure Expansion

Backen, Arragoni & Ross (BAR); The Steinberg Group; ELS/Elbasani-Logan; The SWA Group, landscape architects, 2000–2005

Stanford West Apartments

After more than ten years of political debate as well as escalating costs and redesigns, the multi-faceted project known as Stanford West was initiated. It has included the completion of the Stanford West Apartments (2002) and expansions to the Stanford Shopping Center (2002–2003), as well as the extensions of Sand Hill Road and related infrastructure. The progressive-care Classic Residence by Hyatt

Sand Hill Road

(Senior Housing) project was completed in 2005. Included in the results are the preservation of significant open space and important Native American archeological sites.

151. Mechanical Engineering Research Laboratory

MBT Architecture; Antonia Bava, landscape architects, 2002

The Mechanical Engineering Research Laboratory (MERL) houses research programs that position the mechanical engineering department for leader-ship in critical emerging fields such as advanced manufacturing and design, biomechanical engineering, combustion science, microscale engineering, project-phased instruction, and collaborative research. The warehouse portion of the Press Building was demolished in 2000 to make way for this two-story concrete building, which is set back from Panama Mall and Santa Teresa Street to allow for entry courtyards from both of these major circula-tion corridors.

152. Astrophysics Building

Hoover Associates, 2006

The Astrophysics building is scheduled to be completed in 2006 and will accommodate Dean of Research programs that will be displaced from the High Energy Physics Laboratory (HEPL). The 68,000-square foot structure is designed to be a mirror image of the Gordon and Betty Moore Materials Research building located directly to the south. Two floors above grade will connect to the existing Russell H. Varian Laboratory of Physics building (#47), and the most vibration-sensitive laboratories are accommodated on two basement levels below grade.

Bibliography

Collections

All collections are in the University Archives, Green Library unless otherwise noted.

Collections (call number)

These include the most important collections for the study of Stanford architecture: Arboretum (SC 195); Architecture of Stanford University (SC 125); Roy Ballard (SC 203); John Casper Branner (SC 34); Birge M. Clark (SC 76b) Board of Trustees Supporting Documents (SC 27; SC 282); Peter Coutts (SC 202:1); John Dodds (SC 139); History of the American College Campus (SC 355); Humanities and Sciences (SC 36); David Starr Jordan (SC 58); Miscellaneous University Papers (SC 25); News Service (SC 122); Harry Peterson (SC 107); Planning Office (SC 123; SC 486); Plant Services Office [drawings] (SC 123); Jane Stanford (SC 33b); Leland Stanford (SC 33a); Leland Stanford Collection (SC 512); Leland Stanford Junior (SC 33c); Stanford Family Scrapbooks (SC 33f); Stanford Property Deeds (SC 30); Stanford Ranches and Lands (SC 3); J. E. Wallace Sterling (SC 216); Palo Alto Stock Farm (SC 6); Archibald Treat Correspondence (SC 511); Archibald Treat Photographs (SC 005); Donald Tresidder (SC 151); University Clippings (SC 15); Ray Lyman Wilbur Presidential (SC 64a); and Ray Lyman Wilbur Personal (SC 64b).

Four-Digit File Indexes (call number)

These indexes contain a general and a detailed index, organized by subject matter, including buildings. The most important collections include: Arboretum (0321); Art and Architecture (3590-3629); Art Gallery (3600); Athletics (8500-8999); Board of Trustees Minutes (1101); Bookstore (7570); Birge M. Clark (0756); Buildings (0260); Buildings and Grounds (0200); Campus Planning (0220); Construction—Campus Plan 1885 (0240); Escondido Village (7455); Graduate School of Business (5705); Hoover House (1160); Humanities and Sciences (3620); Landscape Architects (0300); Law School (5035-5065); Mausoleum (0202); Memorial Arch (0290); Meyer Library (6300-6312); Museum (3620); President's Houses (1160); Stanford Barn (9181); Stanford Industrial Park (9170); Stanford Lands Scrapbook (SC 678); Stanford Shopping Center (9180); Stanford West (1270); Terman Engineering Center (3011-3020); and Tresidder Memorial Union (7565).

General Photograph Collection

Planning Office Photograph Collection (PC 62)

Historic Values Index (Stanford's historic buildings with brief historical descriptions)

Drawings and maps collections, listed under Map (M) and Print (P)

Maps and Records, Facilities Project Office (historical and contemporary drawings and blueprints)

Periodicals, Journals, and University Publications

President's Report; Stanford Alumnus (title varies over time); *Stanford Daily; Campus Report; Quad* (yearbook)*; and Sequoia.*

Unpublished Documents (included in above collections)

Ballard, R. P. *History of the Stanford Campus*. 1894.

Final Report of the President's Ad Hoc Housing Advisory Committee. Stanford: 1970.

Mumford, Lewis. *Architecture and the University*. n.p., n.d. [c. 1946.]

———. *Memorandum on Planning*. Stanford: 1947.

———. *Memorandum on Planning II*. Stanford: 1947.

Office of Public Affairs. *Stanford's Proposed Building Plans, 1988–2000*. Stanford: 1988.

Report of Master Plan by President's Advisory Committee on Land and Building Development.
    Stanford: 1954.

Schulz, Henry A., J. D. Galloway, and J. B. Leonard, *Report on Condition of Buildings
    Leland Stanford Junior University , California, and Damages Resulting Thereto
    from the Effects of the Earthquake of April 18th, 1906."* Stanford: 1906.

Skidmore, Owings, and Merrill. *Master Plan for the Stanford Lands*. 1953.

———. Notes on the Interim Report. *Stanford Master Plan*. 1953.

Spencer, Eldridge, *Stanford University Plans and Builds*. Stanford: 1949.

———. *An Over-all Housing Report at Stanford University*. Stanford: 1945 (SC 151, box 15,
    f. 9).

———. *A Student Activities Center for Stanford University*. Stanford: 1956.

———. *An Architectural and Historical Survey of Stanford University Buildings*. Stanford:
    Planning Office, 1949.

———. *Coordinated Plan for the University*. Stanford: Planning Office, 1947.

———. *Studies for Graduate Men's Housing*. Stanford: Planning Office, n.d.

———. *Student Housing Report 1951*. Stanford: Stanford: Planning Office, 1951.

———. *Places to Live at Stanford: A Survey of the Development of Residential
    Accommodations on the Stanford University Campus and Proposals for Adapting the
    Undergraduate Mens [sic] Dormitories to the Proposed House System*. Stanford:
    Planning Office, 1959.

———. *Planning at Stanford. Master Plan*. Stanford: Planning Office, 1952.

———. *Planning Report, Housing 1945*. Stanford: Planning Office, 1945.

———. *Stanford University Plans and Builds*. Stanford: Planning Office, 1949.

[Stanford University]. *Harper's Weekly*, vol. 35, no. 1815 (3 October 1891): 754.

Stein, Clarence. [*Suggestions for the Planning of Stanford University*.] 1951.

The Architects' Collaborative. *Near West Campus Plan*. 1987.

The University and the Future of America. Stanford: 1941.

Tresidder, Donald. *The Next Ten Years*. Stanford: 1947.

Warnecke, John Carl. Housing. *Study of Undergraduate Clusters*. Stanford: 1958.

Secondary Sources

Allen, Peter C. Stanford: *From the Foothills to the Bay*. Stanford, CA: Stanford Alumni
    Association and the Stanford Historical Society, 1980.

———. "The Cottage by the Creek." *Sandstone and Tile* 9, no. 3 (Spring 1985): 3–9.

———. "Memorial Arch." *Sandstone and Tile* 8, no. 2 (Winter 1984): 2–12.

———. "Music Center and Theater." *Stanford Review* 24, no. 2 (February 1958): 33–35.

"Apartments for a College Campus: Stanford University." *Architectural Record* 128 (October 1960): 202–03.

Bates, Bernarr. "Tales from Lagunita Lore." *Stanford Illustrated Review* (April 1934): 189, 208.

Bennett, Paul. "Present Past." *Landscape Architecture* 38 (April 1999): 58–65, 88–93.

Berner, Bertha. *Mrs. Leland Stanford: An Intimate Account.* Stanford: Stanford University Press, 1935.

Betsky, Aaron. "Stanford Recaptures Lost Grandeur." *Architectural Record* (July 1996): 66–71.

"Buildings for Education." *Progressive Architecture* 38 (February 1957): 105–143.

Cannell, Michael. "Recapturing the Pride of Place." *Stanford* (September–October, 1996): 48–55.

Carlton, Eleanor. "Room for Still More Women." *Stanford Illustrated Review* (March 1934): 160.

Casper, Gerhard. *Cares of the University: Five-Year Report of the Board of Trustees and the Academic Council of Stanford University.* Stanford: Office of the President, 1997.

Chandler, Robin. "Always in Style: Stanford University, An Architectural History, 1891–1941." *Sandstone and Tile* 11, nos. 2–3 (Winter–Spring 1987): 6–18.

Chapin, Elise M. "A Brief History of Eight Campus Houses." (1984).

"Charles Coolidge." *Architectural Forum* (May 1936): 66, 68.

Clark, Robert Judson. *The Life and Architectural Accomplishment of Louis Christian Mullgardt.* MA Thesis, Stanford University, 1964.

Clarke, Rosamond. "A New Day for the Five Hundred." *Stanford Illustrated Review* (July 1930): 501.

Dober, Richard. *Campus Planning.* Reinhold Publishing Co.: New York, 1963.

Doty, Andy. "Stanford and Palo Alto After World War II." *Sandstone and Tile* 18, no. 2 (Spring 1994): 13–15.

"El Escarpado." *Stanford Illustrated Review* (April 1930): 348–349.

Elliott, Orrin Leslie. *Stanford University: The First Twenty-Five Years.* Stanford: Stanford University Press, 1937.

"Exercise in Patterned Symmetry." *Western Architect and Engineer* (December 1959): 15–21.

"Farm Houses Spanish Group." *The Stanford Daily* (25 June 1948): 4.

Findlay, John M. *Magic Lands: Western Cityscapes and American Culture After 1940.* Berkeley: University of California Press, 1992.

"Fraternities at Stanford: Simple Shapes Climb a Hill." *Architectural Forum* 119 (July 1963): 110–113.

"Friendly Doors on the Stanford Hills." *Stanford Illustrated Review* 31 (April 1930): 348–349.

Gebhard, David, Eric Sandweiss, and Robert Winter. *The Guide to Architecture in San Francisco and Northern California.* rev. ed. Salt Lake City: Gibbs Smith, 1976.

Historic Houses of San Juan Hill. Stanford: The Stanford Historical Society, 1995.

"Jackstraws Under the Eucalyptus." *Progressive Architecture* (June 1961): 156–159.

"Jewel Library." *Stanford Alumnus* 18, no. 1 (September 1916): 9.

Jones, Frederick W. "Awards." *Architect and Engineer* (May 1935): 11–35.

Jones, Laura, Elena Reese, and John W. Rick. "Is It Not Haunted Ground?" *Sandstone and Tile* 20, no. 1 (Winter 1996): 3–14.

Jordan, David Starr. *The Days of Man*. 2 vols. New York: World Book Company, 1922.

Kirker, Harold. *California's Architectural Frontier: Style and Tradition in the Nineteenth Century*. Santa Barbara, CA.: Peregrine Smith, 1973.

"'Lagunita Court' Built to Meet Every Requirement." *Architect and Engineer* (October 1937): 45–47.

Lerabke, Daryl. "Stanford Fuses Building and Academic Program." *Los Angeles Times*, October 21, 1963.

Linn, Mildred. *Stanford University: Architecture and Ideology*. n.p.: 1964.

Lockwood, Charles. "Mending the Stanford Campus." *Planning for Higher Education* 27 (Fall 1998): 18–27.

McAndrews, Rosemary. "The Birthplace of Silicon Valley." *Sandstone and Tile* 19, nos. 1–2 (Spring, 1995): 3–11.

Miller, Donald. *Lewis Mumford: A Life*. Weidenfeld & Nicolson, New York, 1989.

Mitchell, J. Pearce. *Stanford University, 1916–1941*. Stanford: Stanford University Press, 1958.

"Mumford Envisions Streamlined Farm." *Stanford Daily* 3, no. 15 (February 28, 1947).

"New Architectural Plans for Campus Depicted in 'Stanford Builds' Exhibit." *Stanford Alumni Review* (July 1948): 5–7.

"New Library Building." *Stanford Alumnus* 18, no. 3 (November 1916): 104.

"New Men's Housing Policy Set by Stanford Trustees." *Stanford Review* (April 1957): 15.

"Nathan Cummings Art Building at Stanford." *Art Journal* 29 (Fall 1969): 151–152.

"New and Old on the Campus: Book Store and Post Office, Stanford University." *Architectural Record* 129 (April 1961): 145–148.

Osborne, Carol M. et al. *Museum Builders in the West: The Stanfords as Collectors and Patrons of Art*. Stanford: Stanford University Museum of Art, 1986.

Pearson, Andrew, "Beyond Sandstone and Tile: Defining Stanford's Architectural Style." *Sandstone and Tile* 14, no. 2 (Spring 1990): 1–11.

Pflueger, Milton T. *Time and Tim Remembered: A Tradition of Bay Area Architecture*. San Francisco: Pflueger Architects, 1983.

Porter, Karen. "Lasuen Street, 1898–1957: A Survey of Student Housing." 1981.

"Präsident Hoovers Sommerhaus in Kalifornien." *Die Dame* 52 (May 1, 1929): 7–8.

Press, Harry. "Building 30: The Original Stanford." *Sandstone and Tile* 20, no. 4 (Fall 1996): 10–12.

———— and Roxanne Nilan. "Donald B. Tresidder: The Students' President." *Sandstone and Tile* 15, no. 2 (Spring 1991): 3–9.

Regnery, Dorothy. *An Enduring Heritage, Historic Buildings of the San Francisco Peninsula*. Stanford: Stanford University Press, 1976.

————. "Houses with History." *Stanford Magazine* (Spring–Summer, 1979): 46–51.

"Recent Work of John Carl Warnecke." *Architectural Record* 127 (March 1960): 146–150.

"Respectful Addition to the Stanford Campus." *Western Architect and Engineer* 221 (April 1961): 35–37.

Scott, Mel. *The San Francisco Bay Area: A Metropolis in Perspective*. 2nd. ed. Berkeley: University of California Press, 1985.

"Stanford University Sports Pavilion." *Architectural Record* 119 (May 1956): 175–79.

Starr, Kevin. *Americans and the California Dream, 1850-1915.* New York: Oxford University Press, 1973.

Stone, Edward Durell. "Modern Architecture on the Campus." *Stanford Review* (November 1960): 12–14.

Stone, Wilfred H. "Stanford's House System: The Spaces for Freedom." *Sequoia,* n.d.

Symonds, Allen. *The Row History Project.* Urban Studies Department, 1990.

Temko, Allan. "A Vision Restored." *Stanford* (March 1993): 42–51.

———. "The Humanist Architecture of John Carl Warnecke." *Architectural Forum* 113 (December 1960): 98–107.

———. "Finding Form Once Again on the Farm." *San Francisco Chronicle* February 20, 1978.

"The 1961 AIA Award of Merit: Willow Creek Apartments, Palo Alto, California." *AIA Journal* 35 (April 1961): 84.

"The Center for Advanced Study in the Behavioral Sciences: Wurster, Bernardi and Emmons, Architects." *Arts and Architecture* (February 1955): 13–15.

"The Earthquake at Stanford." *Science* 24 (May 4, 1906): 316.

"The Old Gym and The New." *The Stanford Alumnus* 4, no. 4 (January 1903): 55–59.

"The Oval Changed Beyond Recognition." *Stanford Illustrated Review* 26 (October 1924): 12–13.

"The Saint Gaudens Frieze." *Stanford Alumnus* 3 (1902–1903): 113.

Todd, Ruth. "Sequoia Hall: From Dorm to Demolition." *Sandstone and Tile* 20, no. 4 (Fall 1996): 4–9.

"Trees and Plants and Red Tile Roofs." *Stanford Review* (January 1958): 16–19.

Turner, Paul V. *Campus: An American Planning Tradition.* Cambridge, MA: MIT Press, 1984.

———, et al. *The Founders and the Architects: The Design of Stanford University.* Stanford: Stanford University, Department of Art, 1976.

———. "The Library That Never Was." *Imprint of the Stanford Libraries Associates* (April 1976): 4–13.

———. "The Architectural Significance of the Stanford Museum." In Osborne et al., *Museum Builders in the West,* 92–105.

Thomas Church, Landscape Architect. 2 vols., interviews conducted by Suzanne B. Riess, Regional Oral History Office, The Bancroft Library, University of California, Berkeley, 1978.

Trowbridge, A. L. "The New Entrance Gates." *Stanford Illustrated Review* 33, no. 1 (October 1931).

Warnecke, John Carl. "Stanford's Architecture at the Crossroads." 1949.

Weaver, Sylvia. "A New Dream for Stanford Women." *Stanford Illustrated Review* (July 1930): 500–501, 538–539, 540.

Wells, Bert. "Ready to Double the '500.'" *Stanford Illustrated Review* (June 1934).

"West Coast Microwave Laboratory for General Electric." *Architectural Record* 118 (September 1955): 206–209.

Winslow, Ward. "Tall Trees: The Palo Alto-Stanford Connection." *Sandstone and Tile* 18, no. 2 (Spring, 1994): 3–12.

Specific References by Part

Part One

Allen, Peter C. "The Cottage by the Creek." *Sandstone and Tile* 9, no. 3 (Spring 1985): 3–9.

Bates, Bernarr. "Tales from Lagunita Lore." *Stanford Illustrated Review* 35, no. 2 (April 1934): 189, 208.

Elliott, Ellen Coit. *It Happened This Way.* Stanford: Stanford University Press, 1946.

Jones, Laura, Elena Reese, and John W. Rick. "Is It Not Haunted Ground?" *Sandstone and Tile* 20, no. 1 (Winter 1996): 3–14.

Part Two

Allen, Peter C. "Memorial Arch." *Sandstone and Tile* 8, no. 2 (Winter 1984): 2–12.

Chapin, Elise M. *A Brief History of Eight Campus Houses.* Privately published, 1984.

[Four Curious Bronzes.] *Stanford Alumnus* 4, no. 4 (January 1903): 68.

Historic Houses of San Juan Hill. Stanford: The Stanford Historical Society, 1995.

Hodges, Charles Edward. "The Architects and Architecture of Stanford University." *The Architect and Engineer* 59, no. 3 (December 1919): 115.

Jordan, David Starr. *The Days of Man.* 2 vols. New York: World Book Company, 1922.

Regnery, Dorothy. "Houses with History." *Stanford* (Spring–Summer, 1979): 46–51.

Symonds, Allen. *The Row History Project.* Urban Studies Department, 1990

"The Earthquake at Stanford." Science 24 (May 4, 1906): 316.

"The Old Gym and The New." *Stanford Alumnus* 4, no. 4 (January 1903): 55–59.

"The Saint Gaudens Frieze." *Stanford Alumnus* 3, no. 8 (June 1902): 112–114.

Todd, Ruth. "Sequoia Hall: From Dorm to Demolition." *Sandstone and Tile* 20, no. 4 (Fall 1996): 4–9

Turner, Paul Venable. "The Library That Never Was." Imprint of the Stanford Libraries Associates (April 1976): 4–13.

Turner, Paul Venable. "The Architectural Significance of the Stanford Museum." In Osborne et al., *Museum Builders in the West*, 92–105.

Part Three

Carlton, Eleanor. "Room for Still More Women." Stanford Illustrated Review 35, no. 6 (March 1934): 160.

Clark, Robert Judson. The Life and Architectural Accomplishment of Louis Christian Mullgardt. M.A. Thesis, Stanford University, 1964.

Clarke, Rosamond. "A New Day for the Five Hundred." *Stanford Illustrated Review* 31 (July 1930): 501.

Elliott, Orrin Leslie. S*tanford University: The First Twenty-Five Years.* Stanford: Stanford University Press, 1937

"Farm Houses Spanish Group." *The Stanford Daily* (June 25, 1948): 4.

"Friendly Doors on the Stanford Hills." *Stanford Illustrated Review* 31 (April 1930): 348–349.

"Jewel Library." *Stanford Alumnus* 18, no. 1 (September 1916): 9.

Johnson, Bev. "Branner Hall Tradition Dates from 1944 Change." *Stanford Daily* (March 1, 1956).

"Pedagogy and 'Reflex': Frank Lloyd Wright's Hanna House Revisited." *Journal of the Society of Architectural Historians* 52, no. 3 (September 1993): 307–22.

Jones, Frederick W. "Awards." *The Architect and Engineer* 121, no. 2 (May 1935): 11–35.

"'Lagunita Court' Built to Meet Every Requirement." *The Architect and Engineer* 131 (October 1937): 45–47.

Morrow, Irving F. "Leland Stanford Junior University." *The Architect and Engineer* 59, no. 1 (October 1919): 42–67.

"New Library Building." *Stanford Alumnus* 18, no. 3 (November 1916): 104.

"Präsident Hoovers Sommerhaus in Kalifornia." *Die Dame* 52, May 1, 1929, 7–8.

"Recent Work of Louis Christian Mullgardt." *The Architect and Engineer* 51, no. 3 (December 1917): 39–103.

"Stanford Hacienda Shows Age." *San Jose Mercury News* (November 12, 1964).

"The Oval Changed Beyond Recognition." *Stanford Illustrated Review* 26 (October 1924): 12–13.

Trowbridge, A. L. "The New Entrance Gates." *Stanford Illustrated Review* 33, no. 1 (October 1931): 25, 59–60.

Weaver, Sylvia. "A New Dream for Stanford Women." *Stanford Illustrated Review* 31 (July 1930): 500–501, 538–539, 540.

Wells, Bert. "Ready to Double the '500.'" *Stanford Illustrated Review* 35, no. 9 (June 1934): 255.

Part Four

Doty, Andy. "Stanford and Palo Alto After World War II." *Sandstone and Tile* 18, no. 2 (Spring 1994): 13–15.

Dupen, Douglas W. *The Story of Stanford's Two-Mile Long Accelerator.* Menlo Park, CA: Stanford Linear Accelerator, 1966.

"Exercise in Patterned Symmetry." *Western Architect and Engineer* 218, no. 6 (December 1959): 15–21.

Findlay, John M. *Magic Lands: Western Cityscapes and American Culture After 1940.* Berkeley: University of California Press, 1992.

Lerabke, Daryl. "Stanford Fuses Building and Academic Program." *Los Angeles Times.* October 21, 1963.

McAndrews, Rosemary. "The Birthplace of Silicon Valley." *Sandstone and Tile* 19, nos. 1–2 (Spring 1995): 3–11.

"Mumford Envisions Streamlined Farm." *Stanford Daily* 3, no. 15 (February 28, 1947)

"New Architectural Plans for Campus Depicted in Stanford Builds Exhibit." *Stanford Alumni Review* 49 (July 1948): 5–7.

Press, Harry and Roxanne Nilan. "Donald B. Tresidder: The Students' President." *Sandstone and Tile* 15, no. 2 (Spring 1991): 3–9.

Pryor, Helen B. *Lou Henry Hoover.* New York: Dodd, Mead and Co., 1969.

"Snap Shots of Hoover House." *San Jose Mercury Herald* (November 7, 1928).

Stone, Edward Durell. "Modern Architecture on the Campus." *Stanford Review* 62 (November 1960): 12–14.

Temko, Allan. "Engineering and the Question of Beauty." *San Francisco Chronicle* (October 19, 1966).

Temko, Allan. "Finding Form Once Again on the Farm." *San Francisco Chronicle.* February 20, 1978.

"The Center for Advanced Study in the Behavioral Sciences: Wurster, Bernardi and Emmons, Architects." *Arts and Architecture* 72, no. 2 (February 1955): 13–15.

"Stanford's $20 Million." *San Francisco Examiner* (December 2, 1966): 13.

"West Coast Microwave Laboratory for General Electric." *Architectural Record* 118 (September 1955): 206–209.

Winslow, Ward. "Tall Trees: The Palo Alto-Stanford Connection." *Sandstone and Tile* 18, no. 2 (Spring 1994): 3–12.

Part Five

Allen, Peter C. "Music Center and Theater." *Stanford Review* 24, no. 2 (February 1958): 33–35.

"Apartments for a College Campus: Stanford University." *Architectural Record* 128 (October 1960): 202–203.

"Buildings for Education." *Progressive Architecture* 38 (February 1957): 105–143.

"Fraternities at Stanford: Simple Shapes Climb a Hill." *Architectural Forum* 119 (July 1963): 110–113.

"Jackstraws Under the Eucalyptus." *Progressive Architecture* 42 (June 1961): 156–159.

"New Men's Housing Policy Set by Stanford Trustees." *Stanford Review* 58 (April 1957): 15.

"Nathan Cummings Art Building at Stanford." *Art Journal* 29 (Fall 1969): 151–152.

"New and Old on the Campus: Book Store and Post Office, Stanford University." *Architectural Record* 129 (April 1961): 145–148.

Pearson, Andrew, "Beyond Sandstone and Tile: Defining Stanford's Architectural Style." *Sandstone and Tile* 14, no. 2 (Spring 1990): 1–11.

Pflueger, Milton T. *Time and Time Remembered: A Tradition of Bay Area Architecture.* San Francisco: Pflueger Architects, 1983

"Recent Work of John Carl Warnecke." *Architectural Record* 127 (March 1960): 146–150.

"Respectful Addition to the Stanford Campus." *Western The Architect and Engineer* 221 (April 1961): 35–37.

"Stanford University Sports Pavilion." *Architectural Record* 119 (May 1956): 175–179.

Stone, Wilfred H. "Stanford's House System: The Spaces for Freedom." *Sequoia.*

Temko, Allan. "The Humanist Architecture of John Carl Warnecke." *Architectural Forum* 113 (December 1960): 98–107.

"The 1961 AIA Award of Merit: Willow Creek Apartments, Palo Alto, California." *AIA Journal* 35 (April 1961): 84.

"The J. Henry Meyer Undergraduate Library, and Student Housing Cluster at Stanford University." *Architectural Record* (April 1967): 206–211.

Thomas Church, Landscape Architect. 2 vols. Interviews conducted by Suzanne B. Riess, Regional Oral History Office, The Bancroft Library, University of California, Berkeley, 1978.

Part Six

The Architects Collaborative and the Stanford Planning Office. *Near West Campus Plan.*
Stanford: circa 1987.

Part Seven

Betsky, Aaron. "Stanford Recaptures Lost Grandeur." *Architectural Record* 184, no. 7 (July
1996): 66–71.

Cannell, Michael. "Recapturing the Pride of Place." *Stanford* (September–October, 1996):
48–55.

Casper, Gerhard. *Cares of the University: Five-Year Report to the Board of Trustees and the
Academic Council of Stanford University.* Stanford: Office of the President, 1997.

Press, Harry. "Building 30: The Original Stanford." *Sandstone and Tile* 20, no. 4 (Fall
1996): 10–12.

Temko, Allan. "A Vision Restored." *Stanford* 21, no. 1 (March 1993): 42–51.

We would like to thank the staff of the University Architect / Planning Office who gave a variety of assistance, especially Laura Jones, Karin Moriarty, and Marcos Diaz Gonzalez. The staff of the Special Collections, Green Library answered many questions while guiding us through their extensive holdings. Cindy Kirby assisted us in the Office of Maps and Records; and Maggie Kimball, the University Archivist, provided special assistance in reviewing the final draft and providing expert critique. We also want to express our appreciation to our families and close friends who encouraged us in this endeavor of "caring and concern" for our campus.

Richard Joncas, David J. Neuman, and Paul V. Turner, 1999

With the publication of the second edition, I was able to correct a variety of errors and omissions in the first edition, and to add Part Eight to the *Campus Guide*, which incorporates all of the projects begun during President Emeritus Casper's tenure and my time as University Architect at Stanford. In completing this update, I am especially grateful to my longtime friend and associate, Marlene Bumbera, who assisted me in this effort and had earlier been involved in the initial planning for what eventually became the *Campus Guide to Stanford University*.

David J. Neuman, FAIA
Architect for the University of Virginia
March 2005

Index